Pieced By Mother

Over 100 Years Of Quiltmaking Traditions

Jeannette Lasansky

An Oral Traditions Project

Published by the Oral Traditions Project of
the Union County Historical Society,
County Court House, South Second Street,
Lewisburg, Pennsylvania 17837
Copyright © 1987, Oral Traditions Project.
All rights reserved.

Editor, production and finances:
Jeannette Lasansky
Design: C. Timm Associates
Photography: Terry Wild
Typography: Batsch Spectracomp, Inc.
Printing: Dai Nippon Printing Co., Ltd.,
Tokyo, Japan.

Library of Congress Cataloging-in-
Publication Data

Lasansky, Jeannette.
Pieced by Mother.
Published in conjunction with an exhibition
at Bucknell University's Center Gallery,
May 10-June 30, 1987.
Bibliography: p.
Includes Index.
1. Quilts—Pennsylvania—History—19th
century. 2. Quilts—Pennsylvania—History
—20th century. 3. Quiltmakers—
Pennsylvania—Biography. I. Oral Traditions
Project (Union County Historical Society)
II. Bucknell University. Center Gallery.
III. Title.
NK9112.L34 1987 746.9′7′09748 86-28663
ISBN 0-917127-02-1

Cover: Pieced and appliquéd patches./
Private collection and the Huntingdon
County Historical Society.

Although unquilted tops or unassembled
patches for a top are not unfamiliar finds,
collections of women's "sample" patches
are relatively rare. A sample patch collection
represents a woman's or a family's
repertoire of pieced or appliquéd designs.
Each pattern was executed just once—done
to see how pleasing or impossible new
pattern ideas were. They then served as
reference for future projects. The individual
paper pieces or templates required for
making a sample block were sometimes
attached.

The cover was made possible by donations
from: Business and Professional Women's
Club of Lewisburg, Country Cupboard,
Inc., Laurelton Women's Club, Lewisburg
Council on the Arts, Mary Koons Shop,
Mifflinburg Buggy Museum, Packwood
House Museum, Slifer House Museum,
Susquehanna Valley Branch of the American
Association of University Women, and the
Union County Historical Society.

Inside cover: Cardboard and paper quilting
templates made by Mary Elizabeth
Shumaker Stailey b. 1871 Liverpool, Perry
County d. 1947 Liverpool, Perry County./
Stailey collection.

Acknowledgments

This monograph on central Pennsylvania
quilts from Sullivan, Columbia, Montour,
Dauphin, Cumberland, Perry, Juniata, and
Huntingdon counties is the eleventh in a
series that the Oral Traditions has published
since its first on area stoneware
pottery—*Made of Mud*—in 1977. That
project, as well as this one, coincided with
a major exhibition at Bucknell University.
Since that time both the size of the
exhibition and that of the publication have
expanded as have our ideas on what
constitutes solid research and sound
interpretation. Some, who were part of that
first effort, are still working as part of our
research and production team and they
include my daughter, Diana, and my
friends, Elsbeth Steffensen, Wilma Mattioli,
Joan Maurer, and Connie Timm. The
Pennsylvania Council on the Arts helped
fund our first research effort as they have
for every consecutive project for which we
have sought financial support; so has our
parent organization, the Union County
Historical Society. The support of these
individuals and groups over the years has
been especially important.

This is our third in a series of quilt
studies and possibly our final area survey as
we look to other organizations in the state
to undertake the task in their respective
areas—hopefully inspired by our efforts.

Every large effort depends on the
cooperation and hard work of a group of
dedicated people. This project is no
exception. Shirley Bingaman, Emily Blair,
Gloria Braun, Molly Conrecode, Kate
Hastings, Tandy Hersh, Diana Lasansky,
Megan Lewis, Joan Maurer, Martha Root,
Jean Shackelford, Alisha Spinner, Elsbeth
Steffensen, and Sue Taylor comprised the
documentation team that worked with
people and their quilts at the successive
quilt days. Laurene Lozoski, Jennifer Taylor,
and Sue Travis aided us in Dauphin County.
Each county's host organization's work was
crucial in determining the local response
and I would like to extend special thanks
to Resta Tressler and Pauline Whitekettle at
the Perry County Historical Society; to Jane
Marhefka, the home economist at the Penn
State Extension Service in Juniata County;
to William Ryan at the Columbia County
Historical Society and to Eileen Kocher at
the Berwick Public Library; to Clara
Slembarski of the Pennsylvania Quilters; to
Carol St. Clair at the Sullivan County
Historical Society, to Nancy Shedd at the
Huntingdon County Historical Society; to
Charles Sanders at the Cumberland County
Historical Society and to Carl Dickson and
his staff at the Fort Hunter Museum in
Harrisburg. Susan Brady and Louise
Heberling did extensive work with
Huntingdon County inventories.

Others, from around the state and across
the country, told us of central Pennsylvania
quilts and their stories: Sheila Betterton,
The American Museum in Britain, Bath;
William D. Gordon, Associate Archivist,
Pennsylvania Historical and Museum
Commission; Eve Wheatcroft Granick of
Lewisburg; Sue Hannan of Washington, D.
C.; Arlene Kerstetter of Sunbury; Cathryn
McElroy, Curator of Decorative Arts at the
State Museum of Pennsylvania; Bets Ramsey
of Chattanooga, Tennessee; Jack H.
Reichart, Jr., Oakton, Virginia; Nancy Roan
of Bechtelsville, and Shalom Staub, the
director of Pennsylvania's folklife program.

I would like to thank them for their
thoughts and correspondence as well as
those dozens of area families who returned
much-needed genealogical information to
us. And, of course, the effort is endebted to
the Union County Historical Society's "gal
Friday," Wilma Mattioli; readers Martha
Root, Jean Shackelford and Elsbeth
Steffensen, and copy editor, Joseph Foster.

Jeannette Lasansky
May 1987

Note to the illustrations

Each illustrated quilt is labeled with as
much information as possible: the
quiltmaker's maiden and married names,
place and date of birth and death while any
signatures or dates on the quilt are indicated
and whether they are sewn or inscribed.
The general techniques employed in the
quilt are noted as well as the types of fabric
used: cotton—solid-colored, calico, chintz,
or print (being larger figures than in a
calico), silk, wool, et cetera. Any surface
stitching is indicated and whether the piece
is knotted or quilted. The thread color is
white unless mentioned otherwise and the
stitches per inch (counted in three quite
separate places on the top surface) are
acknowledged. All were hand-quilted unless
noted. The batting or filling is not
mentioned. It was presumed to be
commercial cotton batts—unless there was
wear there was no opportunity to fully
confirm this. Most of the heavy haps or
comforts were wool filled. The overall
measurements are exterior ones. The quilt's
present owner is also indicated and a
photograph of the maker, usually an
ancestor, is reproduced when at all possible.

The body copy includes comparative
information when not covered in the
chapter's text as well as additional quilt or
family information. It is here that the sizes
of the pieces, the numbers of them, the
abundance and types of quilting motifs
might be stated if of particular interest.
Pattern names are not emphasized in this
book since the present owner rarely knew
what the maker called the quilt and that
was our interest, not what the pattern is
called now. When the owner had a family
name for the piece it is indicated in quotes.

Plate 1. (opposite) Detail of quilt made by
Hannah Norris Dean b. 1842 Penn
Township, Huntingdon County d. 1917
Altoona, Somerset County. Applied
solid-colored and calico cottons on white
top with white back. Applied solid-colored
binding. 80″ × 84″ with 7-8 stitches per
inch./Collection of Mr. and Mrs. William E.
Cremer.

When Hannah Dean's husband died in 1894
two of her nine children were still living
with her. The older of the two was Eunice
Margaret Zela Dean and she was nearly
twenty. Her mother felt that it was
important that she make Eunice a quilt. It is
seen here inscribed "pieced by Mother."
Eunice never married so the initials on the
quilt remained her's until her death in 1973.

Fig. 1. (opposite) Hannah Norris Dean.

CONTENTS

FOREWORD

Within a year after completing a major quilt research effort in central Pennsylvania, the Oral Traditions Project was contemplating another in surrounding counties: Sullivan, Columbia and Montour to the northeast; Dauphin, Cumberland, Perry, Juniata, and Huntingdon to the south and southwest of the original seven surveyed. "Why?" one asks. With the original research team still available and others eager to join, it seemed logical to continue to extend and refine our efforts. Leads and queries were coming into the office. The need to expand the search for central Pennsylvania's quiltmaking traditions was expressed by a diverse group: owners, collectors, historians, museum people, and quilters.

Also a number of experiences was forcing us to look at quilts and their makers differently than we had done just a year before. No sooner had the exhibition, *In the Heart of Pennsylvania/19th and 20th Century Quiltmaking Traditions*, closed, than the author was working intensely on a survey of New Mexico contemporary traditional quiltmakers with Nora Pickens. The opportunity to head such an extensive effort in a vastly different part of the country permitted comparisons not often available firsthand. Following that was a three-month stay in Minnesota with exposure to their state historical society's fine collection and to the major historical and contemporary quilt show held each year in Winona. Classes at Carleton College with Karal Ann Marling on the "Colonial Revival in America" and on our culture in the 1930s opened up new lines of inquiry. Finally, there was the presentation of scholarly papers on quilt research at the American Quilt Research Group's annual conference in San Rafael, California. The work of Laurel Horton and Virginia Gunn in particular on quiltmaking in the South during the Civil War and the influence of the Sanitary Commission's effort respectively, along with Erma Kirkpatrick's analysis of *The Progressive Farmer's* advocacy of quiltmaking were of particular significance for this author.

The time spent in New Mexico strengthened a latent feeling that the first half of the twentieth century needed to be looked at more intently and soon, while the makers were alive and articulate, and in all parts of the country. The 1920s ushered in a new era in quiltmaking with dramatic changes in fabric, design, and needlework patterns. There were the traditional approaches and patterns, newly designed patterns and attitudes, and the merger of the two. It was a time of looking frenetically both back and ahead, epitomized in the World's Fairs held in Chicago, St. Louis, San Francisco, and New York. "Grandma's quilts" were exalted, displayed, examined, and sometimes bypassed. The Sears, Roebuck quilt contest in 1933, in conjunction with the "Century of Progress" exposition, encouraged both past and new quiltmaking traditions all over the country.

In quilt historians' desire to begin from the beginning in their respective regions, they often get mired down in the origins of the quilts, the evolution of techniques in dyeing and printing cloth, and concentration on the earlier examples only to give short shrift to the late nineteenth and the early twentieth century, a period when the bulk of extant quilts was made. The New Mexican experience suggested the possibility that the reverse might be more rewarding. Start with the older women and their work while one can tap them as a source—a national treasure—and work backwards, not forgetting to consider documenting also the second major quiltmaking phenomenon of our century, the late 1960s until the present, when both traditional and new are being explored with enthusiasm and vigor.

Another gnawing concern nurtured in the Southwest was the need to be always openminded, fresh, and neutral when approaching such research. Certain biases exist based on our cultural baggage. We cannot help being a product of our cumulative experiences but we should work at not letting them get in the way. For example, after having been so attuned to oldtime Pennsylvania quilters' work and their attitudes, especially in regard to a quilt's needlework, the author quickly had to abandon those attitudes when looking at and talking about quilts made in New Mexico. The environment, economy, fabric and design sources, as well as local lifestyle, were different and sparer by far from those of central Pennsylvanians of the same era. Similarly, the historical body of work of central Pennsylvanians, often remote and rural, would have been shaped by a different set of circumstances from that of fellow Pennsylvanians living in Philadelphia, Chester and lower Montgomery counties, close to urban sources.

The need to confront and understand frontier mentality as reflected in construction type, pattern and fabric selection was evident after the Southwest experience. Unfortunately the frontier period in Pennsylvania is beyond our reach either in interviewing the makers or in seeing a large body of extant quilts, but such is not the case in the other areas of the country. Books that help us understand the frontier experience, particularly as it affected women include Joanna L. Stratton's *Pioneer Women/Voices from the Kansas Frontier* (New York: Simon and Schuster, 1981), Lillian Schlissel's *Women's Diaries of the Westward Journey* (New York: Schocken Books, 1982), and Cathy Luchetti and Carol Olwell's *Women of the West* (St. George, Utah: Antelope Island Press, 1982). Quilt projects such as *Lone Stars/A Legacy of Texas Quilts* (Austin: University of Texas Press, 1986) might help us understand those experiences as they were reflected in an area's material culture.

Frontier quilts, no matter where they were made, should share common factors. But, because the frontier period of one location is chronologically different from that of another, the quilts also reflect national trends of that particular era, both in the fabrics available and the designs popular at the time. Within this broad framework one then considers the individual at work: an older, middle-aged, or younger woman whose attitudes are formed by her past and current lives. Thus each quilt is a complex response to a unique combination of circumstances. All the more reason to investigate as thoroughly as possible while we can, the individual, local, regional, and national picture.

The case for research in the twentieth century is compel-

Plate 2. Detail of quilt made by Mrs. Shenk shown on page 6.

3

Plate 3. Quilt made by Mrs. Shenk d. ca.late 1930s Hummelstown, Dauphin County. / Pieced and applied print and calico cottons with print back. Back brought to front as edge treatment. 84" × 94" with 6 stitches per inch in colored thread. / Collection of John Franklin Nesbit

ling. Not only the early twentieth century should be considered but also the disruption of quiltmaking caused by extreme social change in the World War II period; later the influence of the approaching Bicentennial and the formation of quilt guilds, national quilt magazines and by major exhibitions; followed by the new wave of quilt books and historical research based on state and regional projects.

It is also important for those involved in such research efforts to be aware of the potential impact of historical events as they relate to the craft and crafts people being studied. In addition, with quiltmaking, it is revealing to analyze quilts as they mirror women's various and interlocking roles: as nurturers (warm, bright bedcoverings); as communicators (friendship and signature quilts, quilts with political or social overtones, quilts with particular personal sorrow or exuberance expressed); as accomplished crafts people (Crazy and prize-winning quilts).

The Industrial Revolution more than any other event made quiltmaking a textile phenomenon of major proportions, as is well illustrated by Rachel Maines in her paper "Paradigms of Scarcity and Abundance/The Quilt as an Artifact of the Industrial Revolution" *In the Heart of Pennsylvania/Symposium Papers* (Lewisburg, PA.: Oral Traditions Project, 1986). First needles, then material, thread, material again, and finally dyes were to be crucial in the flowering of this old textile medium.

It was during the Civil War that quilts were called on in a variety of ways to provide both protection and comfort as well as to raise funds. In the North, not long after militias were formed, women were asked to make supplies and, Virginia Gunn remarks in her paper "Quilts for Union Soldiers in the Civil War," *Uncoverings 1985* (Mill Valley, California: American Quilt Study Group, 1986), door-to-door blanket raids for quilts, counterpanes, and blankets were begun. Women's benevolent societies, by a simple vote, could become soldier's aid societies, and many did so. The call for such supplies was advertised in *The New York Times* on August 3, 1862, and the Sanitary Commission, newly formed for this purpose, was the chief mechanism for supply distribution: "Everywhere throughout the land, in distant mountain vallies [sic], in farm-houses, in city palaces, in the west and on the seaboard the little circle of American women met to ply with nimble fingers the needle for the camp and the hospital. Not being able to risk their own lives, they seemed to feel that too much could not be done for the brave men who were risking all for their common and beloved country. The vast stores of articles, the innumerable boxes of lint, the bales of shirts, drawers and clothes of every kind, the rolls of bandages, the quantities of jellies, wines, cordials and comforts of every description, which have been sent to Washington to the Sani-

Piecing the Quilt

Deep grows the clover, a soft green sea,
Blithely the note of the throstle rings,
And Margery, under the locust tree,
Sits at her patchwork and sews and sings—
Sings and dreams, and her fingers fly,
With sunbeams kissed and with shadows flecked,
And the fair spring hours flit lightly by
With the joy they bring to a bride-elect.

And oh, what a wonderful quilt will grow
Out of those fragments and tiny bits!
And the dimples come and the dimples go,
As she measures and matches, and trims and fits—
A bit of blue in the center there,
From a remnant left of her Sunday gown;
A strip of white and a rose-pink square,
And a border here of chocolate brown—

Chocolate-brown—that was Grandma's dress,
Bought last year when John first came:
Margery's thinking of that, I guess,
For in Margery's cheeks shines forth a flame.
And this is a scrap of Jennie's sacque,
Dots of white on a ground of green,
And tiny, zigzag lines of black,
With drooping, golden bells between.

The sunswept earth is very fair
To the maid who sits in her shady niche,
And a tender thought, that is like a prayer,
Is tightly fastened with every stitch.
There's a new, sweet world that is just at hand,
Where a cozy nest of a home is built,
And she wonders and dreams of that unknown land,
As she sings and pieces her patchwork quilt.

Hattie Whitney/*Good Housekeeping*/March 3, 1888/p. 208

Fancywork

We put ourselves in what we do,
Our brains are in our fingers:
And love leaks dainty labors through,
Like perfume where it lingers.

A useful bit of graceful art
Neath fair hands swiftly growing,
Is of the maker's self a part,
And tells without her knowing.

Odd minutes in a restful place
In peaceful hand employment,
Shall soothe the heart, add many a grace,
And yield your friends' enjoyment.

Mary Gow Walsworth/*Good Housekeeping*/January 1905/p. 411

tary Commission, or to our individual regiments by our women, surpass belief."

Prior to this, in a letter printed April 22, 1861 in *The New York Times*, was the query: I am but a woman, and during these war times, while our gallant sons are flocking to the standard of their country, should be satisfied to stay at home, and take care of the 'babies.' But still, is there nothing for women to do—is there nothing she can do more than this? Although I have done much for my country in this time, cannot some of us volunteer—not to shoulder a musket—but to nurse the sick, bind up the wounded, and render all those little attentions and mercies which a woman loves to do? Suppose a number of us offer our services to attend such and such a regiment, will they accept us, or will we be in the way? We are not afraid of being shot, for Southern chivalry don't harm women, do they? Please call attention to us, and we will respond. Yours, etc., Nightingale

The nightingale's letter was answered with the formation of the Sanitary Commission on June 12, 1861 and seven months later its director, Frederick Law Olmstead, announced in his fortieth report that "Never, probably, was so large an army as well-supplied at a similar period of a great war [75% of regiments had each man provided with one blanket, while 20% has two of inferior quality, while 5% had none]."

Regional branches brought together supplies from small towns and all these goods were stamped by the commission of that region before being shipped where needed most. 1,506 bedticks, 2,564 blankets, 1,177 pillow ticks, 736 quilts, and 1,928 sheets were mentioned as part of a three-month supply by the Commission (January 29, 1865). The supplies, quilts and all, never fully caught up with the need.

To help raise funds for making the Union's supplies, Sanitary Fairs were begun in Chicago, where $78,000 was raised, and they quickly spread to Boston ($140,000) raised, Cincinnati ($250,000), Albany, Brooklyn, Buffalo, New York, Philadelphia, St. Louis, Pittsburgh, and Washington, D. C. They were usually one-to-two-week affairs which pooled the resources of a wide variety of people. An advertisement appeared in *The New York Times* of January 1, 1864 for New York's Sanitary Fair where they hoped to raise over one million dollars: "The miner, the naturalist, the man of science, the traveler, can each send something, that can, at the very least, be converted into a blanket that will warm, and may save from death, some one soldier whom Government suppliers have failed to reach. Everyone who can produce anything that has monetary value is invited to give a sample of his best work, as an offering. . . . Contributions are also invited for temporary loan and exhibition."

In preparation for a similar fair held in Philadelphia that

summer, J. H. Harmon, a lawyer and agent for the Catawissa Railroad, solicited similar contributions and consignments in the Bloomsburg newspaper, hoping that "the people of Columbia [County] and all others desirous to aid in the noble enterprise, for the benefit of our suffering soldiers, will avail themselves of the offer [to have them transported to Philadelphia gratis]." As advertised in local papers, the Philadelphia Sanitary Fair, like its predecessors, wanted to raise money through admission and sales:

PLEASE TAKE NOTICE

The price of a single admission is fifty cents—Children under thirteen half price. This admits to Eighty-one out of the Ninety Departments of the Fair, and to much more than three-quarters of the whole price covered by the buildings. Certain Departments, nine in number, contain articles chiefly for exhibition, and not for sale, have been permitted to charge a separate price for admission as follows:

Art Gallery	.25 cents	Childrens'	
Indian Department	.25 "	Amusement	.25 "
Arms and Trophies	.20 "	William Penn Parlor	10 "
Relics and		Pennsylvania	
Curiosities	.20 "	Kitchen	.10 "
Horticultural		Skating Pond	.10 cents
Department	.25 "		

The Executive Committee assures the Public that although the full money's worth will be obtained from a visit to the eighty-one departments to which the entrance fee admits, yet it will be found that the nine other departments will amply reward the visitors and justify the additional outlay. All must bear in mind that, by these extra charges, the total receipts are increased and the holy cause is as much assisted as it would be, were the same sum expended by visitors in the purchase of articles exposed for sale. (*The Bloomsburg Enterprise*, June 11, 1864).

Quilts were among the needlework objects both displayed in exhibits and sold through raffles. At the old-time kitchen exhibitions at the fairs, quilting was often demonstrated.

Virginia Gunn estimates that over 125,000 quilts were provided to military units through the Sanitary Commission, a figure that she feels might have doubled when one considers those given to family or friends directly. Unfortunately, though we know that quilts played a major role in the Civil War, and were "marked" when sent through the Sanitary Commission, finding actual marked examples is nearly impossible. More frequently found are those Southern quilts hidden from Yankees by resourceful Southern women and now handed down along with their oral tradition. As Laurel Horton mentions in her complementary article on "South Carolina Quilts in the Civil War," *Uncoverings 1985*, (Mill Valley, California: American Quilt Study Group, 1986), there too, more traditional and even old-fashioned textile traditions were revived in this time of need; spinning wheels were brought out of attics and looms as well. However, as the North's blockade of the South became effective, the price of the materials used in making quilts became prohibitive, often being $12-16 per yard and once recorded as high as $125.

Not only during the Civil War were quilts connected intimately with historical events but also during World War I when women were urged to make their own home bedding supply so that commercially-made blankets could go overseas. In September 1918, after numerous articles had appeared in newspapers and magazines saying "Make Quilts—Save the Blankets for Our Boys Over There," *Modern Priscilla* offered four quilt patterns so women could do just that. They were nicknamed "Liberty Quilts" and one was designed to be quilted on the sewing machine, using an attachment that had been invented for that purpose twenty-six years earlier. The Depression, with its numerous W.P.A. proj-

ects like the one documented in Merikay Waldvogel's article "Quilts in the W.P.A. Milwaukee Handicraft Project 1935-1943," *Uncoverings 1984* (Mill Valley, California: American Quilt Study Group, 1985), was also a time when historical events and quiltmaking were interconnected (pp. 18-23).

The evolution of women's role in the home has been the subject of recent scholarship useful as background for quilt researchers. It includes Harvey Green's *The Light of the Home* (New York: Pantheon, 1983), Nancy Cott's *The Bonds of Womanhood* (New Haven: Yale University Press, 1977), C. Kurt Dewhurst, Betty and Marsha MacDowell's *Artists in Aprons* (New York: E. P. Dutton, 1979), Linda Grant DePauw and Conover Hunt's *Remember the Ladies* (New York: Viking Press, 1976), and Susan Burrows Swan's *Plain and Fancy* (New York: Holt, Rinehart and Winston, 1977). Quilt historians such as Cuesta Benbury, Katy Christopherson, Ricky Clark, Dorothy Cozart, Pat Ferrero, Virginia Gunn, Laurel Horton, Bets Ramsey, Julie Silber, and Merikay Waldvogel are among those whose work, in print or film, pursues these issues and their relationship to quiltmaking.

However, it is oral work with individual quiltmakers that transports one from the inescapable abstractness of the printed page, no matter how well researched and composed, to the reality of the woman before you. Not only the words but also her inflections, her facial responses, in addition to her own work, come together in one setting and make possible a more complete understanding of her role within the total picture of quiltmaking. One tries to capture a particular woman's role and her quilt's reflection of it. Hers is an experience that is unique but also represents a larger body of attitudes, such as when Mary Stabnau of Newville, Cumberland County recalls how quilting was popular with the neighbors when she started to learn as a five-year-old (1916). They used mainly remnants from clothesmaking as well as used feedbags (for they raised chickens) and sugarbags for the backs. They all enjoyed material and she admits still "going wacky" over it. Some material had unusual associations. For instance, when Mary was twelve her family learned that a neighbor, a mother pregnant and due momentarily with her sixth child, had just discovered that one of her sons had a severe heart problem. It was the day before Christmas and Mary's older sister, who had just made a Santa suit, put it on, and with her family in tow carrying gifts, waded across the snow-covered field in the suit. They surprised the neighbors and made them happy. Later the family, to preserve the happy memory, made the suit into a quilt.

Like other traditional quilters such as Julia Horting and Gladys Leitzel of Newport and Cocolamus, Perry County, Mary feels that "quilting makes the quilt (and that many don't quilt the way they used to)." Though Mary had only seven quilts in her dowry and makes but two a year, over the years, the numbers have accumulated so that now she can count fifty-two to her credit. The women all remember the quilting bees as being one way to get things done and Julia Horting began at age six to attend (1909) and was then the "errand girl." Those attending a bee were usually neighbors or members of the same church. Poorer quilters were there to get needles ready and do the dishes. Rarely were stitches taken out. In looking back to those days with arrivals beginning at 8 a.m. in horse-drawn vehicles, Julia smiles, "Oh, there was lots of fun to see those ladies all together, talking and laughing, jagging their fingers—more blood there than bloody murder." Yes, quilting, the women agree, is a compelling necessity whether one is making one, two, or many more a year. As Gladys Leitzel sums it up for quilters past and present: "Whenever I see a quilt, I think I have to make it. I don't know if it's a bad habit or what!"

4

Plate 4. Quilt made by Susan Harmon Wolfe b. ca.1870 Loyalton, Dauphin County d. ca.1955 Loyalton, Dauphin County. / Pieced and applied solid-colored and calico cottons with print back. Applied solid-colored binding. 78″ × 86″ with 8 stitches per inch in white and colored threads. / Collection of Evelyn McKeague.

This Dauphin County quilt moved along with its owner, the daughter of the maker, to Renovo, Clinton County in the early twentieth century. When brought to a quilt documentation day in Clinton County several years ago by Susan Wolfe's grandaughter it stood out as atypical. Its strong pallette of orange, brown, and green is seen in areas of Dauphin, Lebanon, Berks, and Lancaster but not in other counties of central Pennsylvania. The pattern is unusual, perhaps one of a kind.

5

Plates 5 and 6. *Quilt made by Fannie Mumma Hershey b. 1832 Hershey, Derry Township, Dauphin County d. 1909 Hershey, Derry Township, Dauphin County. Pieced calico cottons with print back. Back to front as edge treatment. 92" square with 7 stitches per inch. / Collection of Dr. and Mrs. C. R. Brandt.*

Small pieces of purchased quilting calicos comprise each 4¾" block. A bull's eye quilting pattern was done in the small orange sash block as well as in the border. The calicos' pallette is typical of the area in which it was made as are those in Jane Snyder's quilt (opposite).

6

7

Plate 7. Detail of quilt made by Jane Susan Bender Snyder b. 1866 Elizabethville, Dauphin County d. 1927 Elizabethville, Dauphin County. / Pieced print and calico cottons with print back. Back brought to front as edge treatment. 79″ × 90″ with 8 stitches per inch. / Collection of Darla Kaye Buffington.

Fig. 2. *Jane Susan Bender Snyder.*

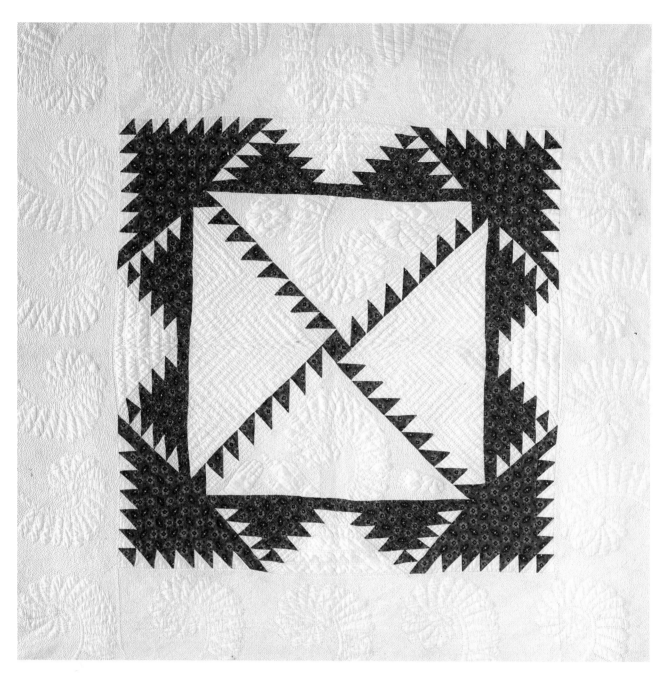

8

9

10

Plates 8-10. *Cumberland County quilt. / Pieced print and white cottons with white back. Back brought to the front as edge treatment. 102" × 95" with 7-8 stitches per inch with rows as close as ⅛" apart. / Collection of Mrs. James D. Flower.*

A superb Cumberland County quilt, this Saw Tooth *is organized in a Central Medallion style. In a note written in 1964 by former owner Jane Smead, she remarked: "The little baby's foot traced in stitching on this quilt is that of my mother's baby brother who died when she was about 3 years old (about 1853). They were the children of James T. Stuart and Martha Jane Woods Stuart. There are also the fingers of two adult hands along the border. I see also his little hand!" Not only the hands and foot but also dozens of fiddle head ferns encircle the pieced motifs. The quilting is exquisite not for its stitches per inch but rather for the eveness of the stitches, the closeness of rows, and the highly unusual as well as personal motifs.*

11

Plate 11. *Quilt made by Lydia McAllister Jacob b. 1785 outside of Newville, Cumberland County d. 1849 outside of Newville, Cumberland County. / Pieced print and white cottons with white back. Applied print binding. 103″ × 105″ with 7-8 stitches per inch with rows as close as 1/8″ apart in places. / Collection of Lydia McCulloch Thorpe.*

Another meticulously quilted and even larger blue and white Saw Tooth *has been considered as "special" by*

the family of Lydia McAllister Jacob. The maker passed it on to her daughter Eleanor Jacob Scouller (b. 1816). Her daughter Lydia Eleanor Scouller Williams (b. 1844) inherited it as did her daughter Eleanor Williams McCulloch (b. 1875). Finally it has come down to Lydia Eleanor McCulloch Thorpe (b. 1902) the quilt's present owner. Like Lucetta Reichart's quilt (opposite), which was made nearly one hundred years later, this is organized as a Central Medallion.

GEVALIA®
Limited Edition
KAFFE

Gevalia® Master Taster Willy Pettersson personally selects your Limited Edition coffees.

Gevalia® *Limited Edition for August 1997*

Coffee: Tarrazu	**Origin:** Costa Rica
Lot: M	**Quantity:** 2,540 bags

Dear Tour Companion:

I am proud to present you with the pride of Costa Rica's small family farms and plantations — extraordinary Tarrazu coffee, your Gevalia® Limited Edition selection for summer.

As the "Sip & Study Notes" on the back of your enclosed Certificate of Authenticity explain, Costa Rica is noted for producing consistently superb coffee. One reason for this is the nation's strong commitment to conservation, with policies designed to preserve and "give back" to the rich, coffee-growing environment. Another reason is the devoted care with which fine Costa Rican coffee like Tarrazu is grown and harvested.

As the Master Taster for Gevalia®, I am very pleased to be able to select from crops that have been so diligently cultivated. As your Certificate of Authenticity attests, the lot I selected consists only of high-grade "Strictly Hard Bean" coffee and is limited to 2,540 bags. To further document that the coffee you have received is genuine Limited Edition Tarrazu, remove the seal from one of your coffee packages and affix it to your Certificate.

After I made my selection, the green Tarrazu beans were shipped to our European roastery and carefully roasted according to my direction. I am sure you will be impressed by the light-bodied, fruity and floral taste of this superior coffee.

Tarrazu is only one of the rare coffees you will enjoy four times a year through the Limited Edition program from Gevalia®. In the months ahead, you can look forward to experiencing these other fine selections:

Antigua from Guatemala (November 1997) Grown at some 4,500 feet above sea level in a high mountain valley cradled by active volcanoes, and nourished in the nitrogen-rich soil created by the ash of their periodic eruptions, Antigua is highly coveted among connoisseurs. Full-bodied yet balanced, with a touch of sweetness, it is one of the most "complete" and satisfying coffees you will ever experience.

Popayan from Colombia (February 1998) This rare Colombian coffee is grown in the country's remote southwestern region, where high elevations make for a mild climate. Combined with the rich, red volcanic soil, the result is a full-bodied coffee with a soothing taste. One sip and you'll understand why some call it the "Bordeaux of coffee."

Chipinge from Zimbabwe (May 1998) Grown on the slopes of Mt. Selinda in Zimbabwe, this unique and exotic coffee thrives in the rich African soil, nurtured by generous tropical rains. At the peak of maturity, the rare beans are handpicked, hand-sorted and prepared with the utmost care at the Farfell Estate, a quality grower and processor chosen by me to supply this exquisite coffee.

I look forward to sharing all these rare Limited Edition coffees with you, including our special selection for the December holidays, Maragogype from Mexico. If you haven't already reserved all five selections, just call our toll-free number: 1-800-GEVALIA (1-800-438-2542). And, by all means, write to me with your questions and comments. I will do my best to answer them and help you get the most pleasure out of your Limited Edition coffees from Gevalia®.

Sincerely,

Willy Pettersson
Gevalia® Master Taster

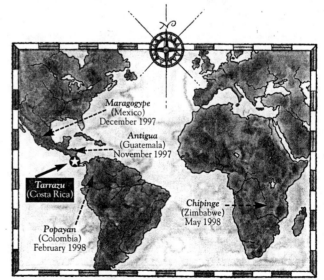

P.S. If you are interested in receiving more Tarrazu or other Limited Edition coffees, it may be possible. Call 1-800-GEVALIA (1-800-438-2542) to see if we have any supplies remaining. As a valued member of this program, you have first priority on any extra Limited Edition coffee in our reserve.

T97L

12

Plate 12. Quilt made by Lucetta
Garrerich Reichart b. 1867 Dauphin
County d. 1946 Dauphin County. /
Pieced and applied solid-colored and
white cottons with solid-colored back.
Back brought to front as edge
treatment. 76" square with 7-8 stitches
per inch. / Collection of Darlene M.
Wagner.

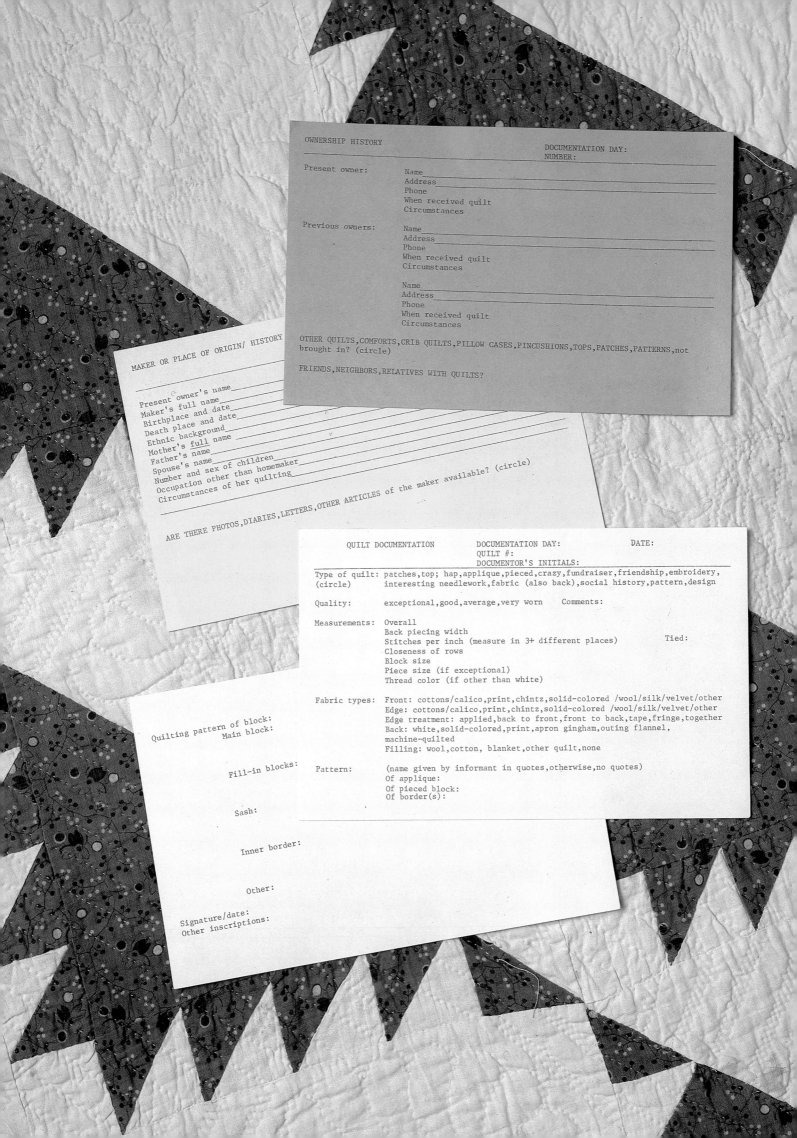

OWNERSHIP HISTORY

DOCUMENTATION DAY:
NUMBER:

Present owner:
Name_____
Address_____
Phone
When received quilt
Circumstances

Previous owners:
Name_____
Address_____
Phone
When received quilt
Circumstances

Name_____
Address_____
Phone
When received quilt
Circumstances

OTHER QUILTS,COMFORTS,CRIB QUILTS,PILLOW CASES,PINCUSHIONS,TOPS,PATCHES,PATTERNS,not brought in? (circle)

FRIENDS,NEIGHBORS,RELATIVES WITH QUILTS?

MAKER OR PLACE OF ORIGIN/ HISTORY

Present owner's name_____
Maker's full name_____
Birthplace and date_____
Death place and date_____
Ethnic background_____
Mother's full name_____
Father's name_____
Spouse's name_____
Number and sex of children_____
Occupation other than homemaker____
Circumstances of her quilting_____
_____

ARE THERE PHOTOS,DIARIES,LETTERS,OTHER ARTICLES of the maker available? (circle)

QUILT DOCUMENTATION   DOCUMENTATION DAY: DATE:
                           QUILT #:
                           DOCUMENTOR'S INITIALS:

Type of quilt: patches,top; hap,applique,pieced,crazy,fundraiser,friendship,embroidery,
(circle)   interesting needlework,fabric (also back),social history,pattern,design

Quality: exceptional,good,average,very worn   Comments:

Measurements: Overall
               Back piecing width
               Stitches per inch (measure in 3+ different places)   Tied:
               Closeness of rows
               Block size
               Piece size (if exceptional)
               Thread color (if other than white)

Fabric types: Front: cottons/calico,print,chintz,solid-colored /wool/silk/velvet/other
               Edge: cottons/calico,print,chintz,solid-colored /wool/silk/velvet/other
               Edge treatment: applied,back to front,front to back,tape,fringe,together
               Back: white,solid-colored,print,apron gingham,outing flannel,
               machine-quilted
               Filling: wool,cotton, blanket,other quilt,none

Pattern: (name given by informant in quotes,otherwise,no quotes)
               Of applique:
               Of pieced block:
               Of border(s):

Quilting pattern of block:
        Main block:

        Fill-in blocks:

        Sash:

        Inner border:

        Other:

Signature/date:
Other inscriptions:

QUILT DOCUMENTATION

A STEP-BY-STEP GUIDE

Quilt documentation days are unpredictable and often hectic sessions but they can be handled smoothly with advance preparation. The following describes in detail how the Oral Traditions Project planned and executed such sessions. While we know that there are many approaches to documentation, we also know that it is helpful to have another research team's methods available when starting out. We found the methods described below to be particularly successful. These procedures have been adapted over the span of two large multi-county projects which recorded thousands of quilts. They will provide a solid foundation for any project that aims to see large numbers of historical quilts and to adequately record them.

Step by step this overview will provide detailed information on the planning and execution of quilt documentation days, including the establishment of contacts, publicity, the physical layout of the documentation site, supplies, the numbering and card system, and photography concerns.

As our research area expanded from the home territory where we had worked on area material culture over a period of thirteen years to outlying counties in central Pennsylvania, we feared that response to our documentation efforts would weaken. That did not prove to be true. The reasons for this are complex but in large part our success was based on advance work that aimed to be thorough and complete.

Establishing Contacts

It is important, as such research efforts go further afield and get larger, that a project work not only with one but a number of appropriate organizations. We found it was very helpful to have a documentation day co-sponsored by the local historical society, the home economist of the Agricultural Extension Service, and women's sewing groups. Granges, ladies aid societies, local museum staffs, and quilt guilds are other groups which could co-sponsor these efforts.

Co-sponsoring meant that the groups agreed to find an appropriate location once we clearly outlined our needs; that they put our press releases in their organizations' newsletters and helped to get proper and repeated coverage in their local newspapers and on their radio stations; that they followed through by watching and listening for this coverage and if it were not forthcoming or entirely correct that they worked to get it right; that they be listed as a local contact for inquiries, and that they knew exactly the parameters of the project, such as the age of quilts being looked at, and provenance, and in this way eliminated misunderstanding and confusion on the day of documentation. (The co-sponsors often had a large body of quilts themselves and people who would serve that day as greeters or runners, helping owners fill out ownership

and maker histories. If knowledgeable, they helped documentors with recording quilts should we be deluged.) Co-sponsors occasionally invited the research team to do a lecture or lecture series on old quilts a month or two prior to the documentation day. Such an event generated additional publicity for the actual research day and again informed more area people about the scope of the research.

Establishing Parameters

Our areas of interest were comforts, quilts, quilt tops, and sample patches completed prior to 1940 and known to have been made by a woman living in one of fifteen central Pennsylvania counties or to have come out of an old area home at auction. In those cases where the newspapers, newsletters, radio, or word of mouth conveyed this information accurately *and* completely we did not find ourselves having to turn away recently-made quilts or quilts from out of the region; this proved to be exceedingly helpful. If people came with quilts from another area, we recorded their name, address, phone number, and the source of their quilts for future reference.

After much trial and error, we found that planning the documentation day effort for a Sunday afternoon produced the most consistent results—usually 150-200 quilts brought in by 60-75 families and individuals. People could come from 1 P.M.-6 P.M. and they usually arrived early (12:30 was common) but rarely came as late as 5:00. They came in family groups since on a Sunday it was treated as a family outing and this proved helpful as often a combination of people contributed to knowledge of the quiltmaker or the circumstances of the making of the quilts. For those who came thinking that they would see a quilt show, we prepared a statement that clarified what we were actually doing that day. It also helped those who came remembering a little but not all of what the local press release had said:

What's Happening Here?

This is not a quilt show or sale but rather an in-depth research effort being conducted by the Oral Traditions Project of the Union County Historical Society and hosted by your county historical society, library, home economist, etc.

People have been asked to come with their old quilts, comforts, tops, pieces, and patches—objects which were made by local women prior to 1940 for the home, family and friends. The project personnel ask owners about the makers when known, about the ownership history of their quilts, and take down information about the piece—such as measurements and fabric type—and take study photographs. They hope to see about 1,500 quilts in an eight-county region: Sullivan, Columbia, Montour, Dauphin, Cumberland, Perry, Juniata, and Huntingdon counties.

Plate 13. Color-coded cards used to record information about each quilt as it was seen.

Next year, this non-profit group will publish a book on our area's quilts and have a major exhibition of about 150 of them at Bucknell University starting May 10, 1987 as well as a three-day national symposium on quiltmaking traditions. They have already published two books on area quilts.

Today is a day when important information is being asked for and exchanged.

Site Concerns

In order to accommodate our staff of ten to twelve, the co-sponsor's staff or volunteers as well as the quilts and their owners, a large church social room proved best for our purposes. Since our efforts were on Sundays, it usually meant that we arrived around noon and moved into the social room to arrange tables and chairs just as soon as the church members left—some staying on with their quilts. Signs directed people into the correct door and out another if possible to provide easy traffic flow. At the entrance there was a series of tables that were usually staffed by members of the co-sponsoring organizations. The first table had desk copies of our publications for people to examine, the handout that stated "What's Happening Here," information on additional quilt documentation days and the forthcoming show, the signup sheet for those who brought quilts from out of the area, and the registration tags.

Each family or person bringing in quilts was given a numbered registration tag that would be keyed into all their quilts, the documentation cards that would subsequently be filled out and the study photography. It was essential that the greeter ascertain if the person had quilts from one or several owners. If the quilts represented more than one owner, they received the corresponding number of tags. Families would then go to those tables located directly behind the greeters and with the help of local volunteers, they would fill out the pink owner card and yellow maker card, and then wait for a documentation table to be free in order to have their quilts recorded on white documentation cards. At that juncture a volunteer was stationed, ready to call registration numbers as documentation tables became available.

It proved best to arrange the documentation tables so that they followed the sides of the room. We preferred large-size tables that were often in these social rooms. Before we began we made sure that the tables were clean and free of anything that might snag a quilt. Only one documentor would be at a table, unless there was a new team member who was training. The documentors would be seated with their backs to the wall, facing a group of two or three chairs on the other side of the table. We learned to put several chairs there to accommodate the different family members and/or their quilts since some families brought as many as two dozen.

Supplies

The documentors had at their table (as well as at a resupply table) the following: 1. pencils only–no pens; 2. a cloth measuring tape; 3. additional copies of the owner card, the maker card, and many quilt documentation cards (these cards are reproduced on p. 16), 4. stamped, self-addressed envelopes to give to those families who could find out more about the

Plates 14-17. These quilt posters, published by the Works Progress Administration (W.P.A.) in South Langhorne, Pennsylvania in the late 1930s or early 1940s, were recently discovered. There are thirty designs in all, silk screened in multiple colors on 20" × 15" oak tag. Some of the posters show a complete quilt, others a quarter panel, and all include a line diagram of the pieced or appliquéd block as well as the pieces needed complete with seam allowance. Some show an alternate use of fabrics but none explain how to do

14

maker and were willing to send in a more complete maker card later on; 5. 2″ × 2″ yellow "post-it" adhesive notes to attach to any of the cards when it was necessary to bring attention to a particularly interesting social history, pattern, a remark on condition, et cetera, and on very busy days, to count but not document certain quilt types (standard *Flower Gardens* and *Double Wedding Rings,* for example); 6. the white tags that would be numbered and lettered, then temporarily attached to a quilt's corner with a small brass safety pin.

The Numbering System

Our documentation system depends on the correct numbering and labeling of the quilts and their series of color-coded cards. This process of information gathering begins with the volunteers at the first tables, and then is confirmed and elaborated on by the documentor at her table. Time and concentration are necessary to make sure that this numbering is done correctly.

For example, an owner approaches the documentor with her quilts, the number which was assigned as she entered, and the owner and maker cards she filled out for her quilts which are keyed into the assigned registration number. If two owners are together and want to stay together that afternoon, they should have been given two separate registration numbers. Sometimes one person will have brought the quilts of several friends or neighbors and consequently have several numbers (one for each owner).

The documentor first needs to make sure that the assignment of the numbered registration tags by the greeters and the subsequent filling out of the owner and the maker cards with the assigned number is complete. If not, additional registration tags and cards should be obtained from the greeter's table before further processing.

The documentor then separates each owner's quilts in piles by maker and/or by the different circumstances of ownership history—auction, gift, purchase, et cetera. This step helps confirm that the already filled-out ownership history cards and the maker cards are correct, or in adding other information. (We used large colored index cards to help us differentiate between the different cards during the day.)

In the simplest of situations there was just the present owner who knew nothing other than that the quilts had been bought at a local sale; in that case only one owner card was filled out. Then the documentor proceeded to document each quilt, filling out separate documentation cards for each—labeled #6a-e for instance. Quilt #6a would have its card (see p. 16) filled out completely by the documentor and have a numbered and lettered tag then pinned to one of its corners; quilt #6b would be next, and so forth.

However, if the owner had quilts made by two different makers as well as one bought at sale, the one from the sale would have only an owner card and no maker card, while the others would have maker cards filled out as well. If Aunt Lydia made two quilts they would be done next, numbered and labeled #6b and #6c, while two quilts made by Grandma Jones would be #6d and #6e. These letters would also be noted on the maker cards.

Sorting out the quilts into the appropriate groupings before launching into the quilt documentation cards is well worth

the block nor is there an accompanying manual. Many of the posters include not only the name of the pattern but also a date and location (not necessarily Pennsylvanian) presumably of a quilt that was copied. The posters were probably used in the Museum Extension Project as a visual aid, or in the 1,451 community centers in Pennsylvania that were affiliated or run by the W.P.A. and which included arts and crafts programming. / Collection of Shippensburg State University.

15

the time taken, as it clarifies the process from the beginning. If care and time is not taken in the beginning, the recording of information can become hopelessly confused. Different ownership histories of quilts owned by the same party can be accommodated by filling out additional owner cards in order to reflect that or by amending a single ownership card (though the former seemed best to us).

It is important to fill out all the cards as completely as possible. Names must be spelled correctly—not phonetically. Be sure the quilt day date and the quilt's *entire* identification number (number and letter) is on every card including maker cards that are being sent home with the owner. Every quilt will end up with a number as well as a letter such as #6a, #6b, #6c, #6d, #6e. The number later tells us the owner and keys into the owner card, but the letter identifies a specific quilt of that particular owner and keys into the quilt documentation cards as well as any maker cards when the maker is known, as in the case of Aunt Lydia for #6b and #6c. The quilt documentation day, both location and date, must be indicated on each card. There will be a 6a from a subsequent documentation day and one needs to be able to differentiate these occasions many months and years later. So, a card needs to indicate "Perry 6a" as opposed to "Juniata 6a." These numbers will be recorded by the photographer who is working on the quilt later and by the office staff much later when the processed film returns. *Correct numbering at all stages is of the greatest importance.* This numbering system, both of cards and quilt tags, does allow for quilts to be separated from their cards (which happens) and to move rapidly and accurately throughout the process.

Quilt Documentation Cards

We refined the quilt documentation cards as they were used, over a number of sessions. They seem logical and "bare bones" to us but to someone else there will be something out of sequence or missing, so you should make the necessary changes to suit your project and circumstances. More research could be done on any given quilt than is indicated by our series of questions and for Album, Fundraising, or Crazy quilts we went on to record more on the cards' backs. The cards were sufficient, however, for the vast majority of the quilts we saw and were manageable on days when we were seeing great numbers of quilts. The cards were abbreviated for quick response (circling an answer rather than writing it out) and areas of inquiry were grouped together for efficiency as well, i.e. all questions that required measurements are together as are fabric concerns, quilting patterns, and so forth. Preparatory sessions on use of the cards were held for the documentors.

Photography

Once all the cards were filled out for each quilt and all of one owner's quilts were completed, the owner was directed to the photography area. That was the final step that day. The principal researcher/author was also the photographer and in this way was able to see all the objects firsthand. Photography needed to proceed efficiently and quickly as this was where—especially on busy days—delay could occur. While the photographer had little to do in the beginning, she was busy throughout the afternoon and would still be at work long after the other members of the documentation effort were finished. Members of the co-sponsoring organizations often helped by holding quilts or placing them in a quilt photography frame. They also kept a list of those who were waiting and would call for the next person when the photogra-

pher was free. Chairs were arranged so that people waiting could, without moving, see the other quilts being photographed. It was preferable that the photography be done in an area that was separate but contiguous to the rest of the documentation effort. On very busy days it might be necessary to have a second photographer for those few hours that became especially busy.

When the quilts were ready to be photographed the cards were looked at quickly and then put in a file box. The photographer, having previously labeled sheets of a long yellow pad A-Z (and #1-36 on each) would enter the number of each quilt being photographed next to the appropriate number(s) on the roll. The number would be taken from the tag attached to the quilt which the photographer would detach and put aside when photography began on the piece. Quilts did not have to be shot in any particular sequence.

For example if the photographer was just beginning on roll "A" (also sheet "A") and if three shots were taken of quilt #6b then #6b would be entered on sheet "A" lines 1-3. If the next quilt was #6e and it was shot only once (as an overall) then #6e would be entered on sheet "A" line 4, and so on. It was important that the photographer label the exposed rolls "A" and so on as they were taken from the camera, and when having them processed, to have the roll's letter put on the processing envelope.

When the processed film was returned it corresponded to the yellow sheets on which the quilt numbers were entered in the order in which they were shot (and which, in turn, corresponded to the appropriate owner, maker and quilt document cards). Slides were then labeled with the name or code for the day as well as the quilt number and attached to the appropriate series of cards for that quilt. Thus, if any one of the cards or slides got separated, they would be reassembled without confusion or mistake.

Exchanging Information

We viewed the documentation days as times to exchange information. The quilt owners shared what they knew of the quilts' ownership and makers (often sending more information, particularly about the quiltmaker, to the project's office later) and the documentors, while recording what they saw in handling the quilts shared their knowledge: dating information, pattern type or style, the piece's rarity, thoughts on care and conservation.

Owners were usually eager to learn more about dating unless, as was sometimes the case, it made the quilt considerably newer. They often wanted to know its worth. We avoided answering with an appraisal value talking instead about how the value was greatest to their family regardless of condition, pattern, execution, or date, and that, if at all possible, this is where the piece should remain. We told them of the price of newly-made quilts of that type and how purchasing one for a grandchild for instance would have none of the historical or familial significance of the piece they presently owned. We talked about how selling to a dealer would give them only a fraction—maybe as little as half—of what its average value was, and that selling at auction could be risky. If there were no descendants and they seemed at a loss of what to do, we talked about a donation to a museum or historical society within the region in which the quilt was made and the benefits that would result. In short, we said, "do not sell!"

We were careful about offering information about pattern type until the owner had first told us what she knew and then we might confirm or add to that. Often we placed the quilt within the overall range of quilts we had been seeing so the owner might know whether it was highly unusual, a very personal rendition of . . . , typical of . . . , and so forth. We always could find something to say about the piece as we were handling it thus allowing the owner to go home with more understanding of the piece's fabrics, needlework, pattern arrangement, and design type.

Care, Conservation and Use

Advice on the care, conservation, and use of old quilts is where we felt we could offer the most to the owners. We tried to reinforce those who are handling their heirlooms correctly and make suggestions to those who, usually unknowingly, were not. Never have we had owners not receptive to our concerns and advice. We usually told them of two recent articles on the subject which we feel are written realistically for those quilts retained in homes: Virginia Gunn's article, "The Display, Care, and Conservation of Old Quilts" in *In the Heart of Pennsylvania/Symposium Papers* (Lewisburg, PA.: Oral Traditions Project, 1986) and Patsy Orlofsky's "The Collector's Guide for the Care of Quilts in the Home," in *The Quilt Digest* (San Francisco: Kiracofe and Kile, 1984).

The most common questions were about the cleaning of quilts—a point on which everyone is more conservative these days. We urged people not to dry clean or wash their old quilts in a traditional manner but to follow the advice given in the Gunn and Orlofsky articles. We urged them to use or display their quilts in a more conservative manner so as not to require cleaning as a result of that use and to be able to accept the fact that many old quilts will have marks of age. We mentioned how, historically, quilts were aired more than washed. Indeed, washing was done once a year at most.

The issue of storage often came up because the owners often brought the quilts in a plastic bag, which is, of course, fine to use that day for protection from a sudden rain but not acceptable for longterm use since the plastic does not breathe and can capture and hold moisture. We urged storage in a clean white sheet and told the owners not to fold the quilt as our mothers and grandmothers taught us to fold bedding—in quarters. Often we pointed out deep crease marks that were already formed by the repeated folding of the quilt in this manner. After photographing their pieces we showed them how, by refolding in thirds, this can be avoided. Also, we urged them not to store quilts piled on top of each other causing stress on the fabrics as well as the needlework.

Fabric rot, especially with some silks and dye-eaten colors, was also addressed. The owners were then knowledgeable of what was happening to their quilt and what they could and could not do about it. Putting a fine netting over areas where the silk was shredding or areas where heavily painted Victorian motifs were cracking was advised. Often we have been

Did you ever know anyone who collected specimens of quilting? Neither did I. There may be people who do, and somewhere there may be a collection of it comprising all the varieties of this ancient and honorable art. Some day there may be an exhibition of it, and may I be there to see! Meanwhile I come upon an occasional example in a museum or an antique shop. One friend may have an ancestral piece which she treasures, while another uses hers for a mattress pad and expends her collecting zeal on pressed glass or patchwork quilts. For collectors of patchwork are almost as common as the quilts themselves, and they are thicker than blackberries. Almost anyone can find patchwork anywhere.

But a collector who likes real sport, who prefers a long hunt after rare game to knocking over a barn-yard fowl, will pass by quilts and trail the lovely and elusive work of the quilting artist. A wary bird it is. You will hear of it often, but it will generally turn out to be something else. I was told of one the other day, a wonderful counterpane with a tree growing from the bottom to the top, all in quilting. But tracked down, the tree proved to be on chintz! There was quilting on it, but it was a minor matter, as it always must be, on a patterned surface. Even when the work done by the quilter is far finer in design and craftsmanship than that of the patchwork, it is overshadowed by it. "The Quilting Quest" by Helen Bowen / *House Beautiful* / January 1924 / p. 43

Two red and white quilts, left to me by a great-aunt, were for many years packed away in a chest in the attic and saw the light of day only at house-cleaning times. When they were hung on the line to air, I always admired the exquisite needlework and the quaint and intricate designs worked out so carefully, with the tiny blocks and diamonds of snowy white muslin and bright scarlet and black calico. Each year we tried to fit them into our bedrooms; but red just would not harmonize with the soft colorings of blue, rose, and mauve that had been so carefully blended. So the quaint old quilts were regretfully but invariably laid away in their hiding place in the attic—perpetual white, or rather red, elephants on our hands. "Red Quilts" by Elsie Marsh Brandt / *The House Beautiful* / October 1926 / p. 656

The Quilting of Old Tops

The recent quilting of old tops became one of our biggest concerns and over the past few years, the project's staff has evolved a strong position. We feel that when a family comes in with a series of tops, they should be made aware of the issues involved in having them quilted. Often they have already had one or two done. There were many women—both in this century and last—who stockpiled patches and tops, some hoping to but never getting around to quilt them all. And then, there were those who just were piecers of patches and tops.

We point out that in having the top quilted, it probably means that they intend to use it as a traditional bedcovering. We bring their attention to the fact that in washing the top when quilted, they might be in for some unpleasant surprises, since the fabric may disintegrate and may not be colorfast. (Even if that does not happen, a top made of old fabrics by being washed would be subjected to wear that should be reserved for new, hardy fabrics.) We urge them to care for, show, and perhaps use the piece just as a top. If they are determined to have it with a "finished" look we ask them to consider the possibility of just turning the top's edge under and lightly basting it or applying a narrow binding. It is the urge to finish an unfinished project and to make it useful that prompts most owners to do something, so we try to set that need in perspective. The consequence of use, the alternatives of highly selective use, and the fact that the piecer may have been satisfied with the piecing itself, help the owners in making their next decision.

One day, after seeing a number of unusually beautiful mid-nineteenth century appliquéd tops that had just been quilted, we set off on another tangent. These were all pieces which if left unquilted, would have been in this book or exhibited as mint 1850s specimens. Now they were neither pieces of the 1850s nor of the 1980s. The use of contemporary high-pile polyester batting and "the look" it creates when quilted was inconsistent with the age of the top. Even though good contemporary quilters had been selected in each case to quilt the old tops, neither the amount of

needlework nor the quilting patterns chosen were appropriate to the way that top would have been quilted had it been done earlier. Each period of time—the early-, mid- or late-nineteenth as well as the early twentieth century—had different approaches to quilting. Good quilters in 1987 would not, under ordinary circumstances, quilt in the manner of a mid-

rewarded by later seeing that same quilt selectively covered, its patches secured in this manner. Again, using Virginia Gunn's article as a reference, we talked about going into repairs slowly and conservatively, never eliminating but rather covering the original fabric with a suitable replacement.

nineteenth century woman. The aesthetic and historical values of the pieces were hurt, not to mention the monetary value.

Barbara Brackman in her timely article on the subject *(Quilters' Newsletter,* May 1986, pp. 26-27) points out, however, that it might be appropriate for a family member to quilt a top that had been done by an ancestor, maintaining a sense of continuity. This is an interesting and valid point as long as all the other factors are considered such as fabric condition, other uses for the top, the intention of the maker (was she a piecer or quilter?), et cetera. If the family decides in that case to proceed to quilt, it might be a challenge to find a batting that approximates the correct look of the top's period and to choose period quilting motifs as well. This is not difficult to do for quilt tops made in the 1920s and 1930s. Crazy quilts and Log Cabins similarly would be a modest challenge. It is, however, those tops from the 1860s and earlier that probably should be maintained as tops since their batting and quilting were so radically different from what is available or being done by quilters now.

These are the kinds of issues we confronted and which any similar research effort will need to think out with the owners as they come in to share their quilts.

Other Documentation Efforts

It is helpful to be aware of other quilt documentation efforts—their standards and objectives, the compatibility of research efforts, in addition to issues concerning longterm and multiple use. Too often we are shortsighted and record only the information we think we need for a particular project only to find out toward the end that we should have thought about more issues and gathered more information. We all work within time and financial constraints, however, and few are given the luxury of no limits so decisions have to be made on such concerns as to how much oral history should be done, the project's quantity and quality of photog-

raphy, for instance. As long as those involved are aware of the issues that are commonly faced in such efforts, they can discuss them, debate them, and finally decide on their project's limits and concerns before proceeding.

The Oral Traditions Project is tempted to continue documenting quiltmaking traditions in other parts of Pennsylvania and we have been urged to do so by others. But rather than spread out too thin and too far from home, it is time to encourage others to proceed in their respective territories, using the results and methods of projects such as ours in central Pennsylvania; also of Bets Ramsey and Merikay Waldvogel's effort in Tennessee, Betina Havig and Suellen Meyer's projects in Missouri, Laurel Horton and Lynn Robertson Myer's in South Carolina, Karoline Bresenhan and Nancy Puentes' in Texas, as well as others underway or being completed in California, Ohio, and North Carolina. It was very helpful to our second project's success to show what we had done in our first, *In the Heart of Pennsylvania/19th and 20th Century Quiltmaking Traditions* (Lewisburg, PA: Oral Traditions Project, 1985). Those starting off fresh could show local people such projects especially if an exhibition and/or publication are part of the overall plan.

Followup

Following each documentation day our documentors met to make their comments on and evaluations of how the day had proceeded, whether there were any patterns or peculiarities to the pieces seen, and then to view all the slides, often seeing for the first time what the documentor right next to them had handled that day. The ability to look at some larger collections of area quilts such as that of the State Museum of Pennsylvania in Harrisburg or to go to a major exhibition like Winterthur's "Quilted for Friends/Delaware Valley Signature Quilts 1840-1855" enlarged the documentors' vision and allowed them to contrast what we were seeing out of area

16

homes in great numbers to selective groupings from other regions.

Also, following each documentation day, a press release was sent to the same local newspapers that had promoted the session. As indicated in the following example, the release would give a synopsis of the day's event and tell of any subsequent documentation days to which additional area quilts might be brought:

Area Quilts Come Out of Blanket Chests

Over 160 old quilts and comforts were brought by area families to a quilt documentation day held at the Blue Ball Tavern in Little Buffalo State Park, outside of Newport. The Perry County Historical Society under Resta Tressler's supervision was host to the Oral Traditions Project of the Union County Historical Society as they were documenting area quilts for a future book and major exhibition scheduled for the spring of 1987.

Nearly fifty families from Landisburg, Marysville, Camp Hill, Harrisburg, Mechanicsburg, New Bloomfield, Newport, Millerstown, Duncannon, Loysville, Carlisle, Hummelstown, and Elliotsburg brought from one to twenty-five quilts each. Martha Rice, Edith Noll, and Fae Cupp won a book, *In the Heart of Pennsylvania/19th and 20th Century Quiltmaking Traditions,* for bringing in the greatest number of quilts while Mary Anne Leiter received a prize for the best documentation, Ralph Smith for the most unusual, and Jerry Clouse for the most typical. Runnersup John Nesbitt for the most unusual, Pauline Whiteketle for the most typical, and Janette Albright and Mrs. Herman Kinter for their documentation will receive a gift certificate toward the purchase of a forthcoming book which will feature Perry, Cumberland, Dauphin, Columbia, Montour, Sullivan, and Huntingdon county quilts.

Area residents are urged to bring more quilts, comforts, tops and patches to the next documentation day which will be held next Sunday from 1-6 P.M. at the Messiah Lutheran Church in Mifflintown. People are encouraged to come anytime during those hours.

The Oral Traditions Project is part of the Union County Historical Society and has published ten books on Pennsylvania craft traditions since 1977. They have received state and national grants to do this work and have won four national book awards for their efforts. The book on area quilts is their next effort.

The next documentation day is being co-sponsored by the Juniata County Historical Society, president, Ruth Waters, and Penn State Extension Service for Juniata County home economist Jane Marhefka. Any questions can be answered by calling Jane at 436-8991 or Jeannette Lasansky at the Oral Traditions Project at 524-4461, ext. 56.

Conclusion

Then came the time to select those pieces that would be photographed for the publication and others which would be in the exhibition. Reference would constantly be made back to the documentation cards and study photography. Cards would be shuffled and reshuffled as the ideas presented by the objects were refined. (Although our project has not gotten to the point of entering information into computers we were aware of our statistics as they related to pattern type, methods employed, et cetera. Definitely, more should be done in this regard.)

We did not want to lose sight of the quilts as useful and usually very beautiful objects made by people and for people. So in selecting those several hundred from several thousands we tried to keep constantly in mind what was typical of our area and to show the best of the typical—the *Variable* and *Lone Stars,* the well organized *Double Nine Patch,* the red and green on white appliqués, the organized Crazy quilts often put together as haps or comforts, the numerous and varied fundraising projects as well as the pink and green calicos and the ubiquitous Turkey red embroidered turn-of-the-century pieces. Without the documentation days based on the mutual cooperation and the sharing of hundreds of area families we would not have been able to say "This is the best of what's typically central Pennsylvania. Enjoy."

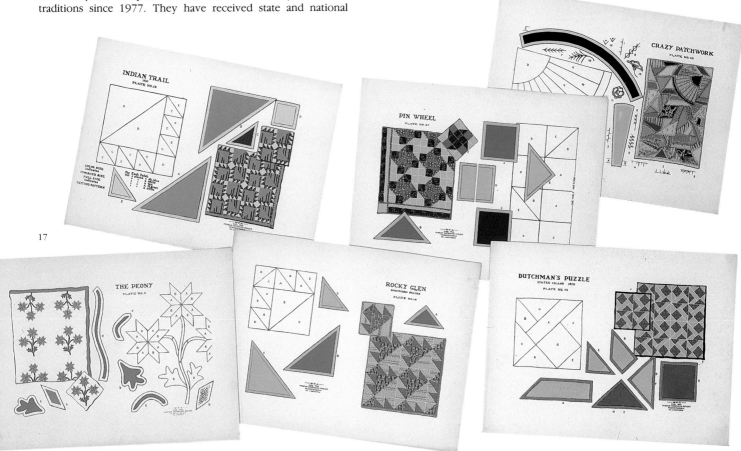

Plain
&
Fancy

Harriet Hill Knorr was three years old when she was introduced to sewing and domesticity, first learning to connect cloth strips for making rag carpets and to assemble four 3″ squares for her first quilt patches. She sewed on her grandmother's lap as the older woman continued to cut out patches. She was taught to "do it right" with her mother and grandmother checking her stitches and many a block was ripped out twice in the beginning. By the time she was five, she was working on her second quilt—what she calls a *Patch on Patch.*

Even at an early age, Harriet was buying new material with one of the six cents she had been given each week for penny candy and ice cream. On Saturday when she went to the local store, she would use a penny to purchase two to three inches of printed cotton material. Sewing came naturally to the little girl who, like many others her age, enjoyed doing most what her mother and grandmother did. They sewed a lot making the family's clothes, and for others. Besides, Harriet lived "way out" in the country and with no one to play with, it felt good to piece, sew, and play with her dog. So, each winter Harriet, along with her mother and grandmother, would make a quilt—a *Patch on Patch,* a *Nine Patch,* or *Four Square.* By the time she was seven, she quilted her first quilt and was quilting with the local Ladies Aid. She began making quilts for her dowry in 1918 and they included her perennial favorites as well as a *Nine Patch* "put together like rickrack," a *Basket,* two Crazy comforts and a Log Cabin. In contrast to Harriet, her sister, who did not like to sew, had only one quilt in her dowry chest. Quilts for the spare bed would be "nicer"—Harriet notes a *Rising Sun* or a *Double Irish Chain* (and a woven, dated coverlet in the winter). At age ninety-one she still quilts with "twenty-five on the way." She can do an "ordinary" quilt in three weeks.

The straightforward, utilitarian quilts and comforts that Harriet Knorr and other central Pennsylvania women—like Martha Hanawalt, Grace Leitzel, and Mary Stabnau—have

quilted form the bulk of central Pennsylvanians' efforts: the *Nine Patches, Double Nines, Expanded Nines, Rail Fences, Album Patches, Irish Chains, Triangles, Bear Paws, Delectable Mountains, Ocean Waves, Lady of the Lakes, Drunkards Paths,* and *Robbing Peter to Pay Pauls* along with the *Flying Geese, Union Squares, Baskets,* and *Churn Dashes.* Mary Hanawalt like Harriet Knorr never made an appliqué which one called "fancy work." For, as this older quilter said, "they took extra time and patience" and when you were trying, as Mary Hanawalt's family did, to make about thirty each year, it worked best to stay with old favorites like the *Irish Chain,* the *Rocky Road to California* or the *Album Patch*—on which other young people would come in to help, putting their name in the block's center.

Though area women consistently reinforce a notion of "plain" versus "fancy," of utilitarian versus "just for show" in their quiltmaking, it should be noted that their concept of plain and utilitarian is different in degree from what is considered plain in some other parts of the country. In Pennsylvania where the nineteenth century, "the golden age of quilt production," is not really a frontier or primitive period—"plain" does not mean quilts made out of good parts of old clothes, of reworked used fabrics, of tops made solely of sewing scraps, feedbags, sugar-, flour-, or tobacco-sacks. "Plain" does not mean rudimentary sewing where five quick, uneven stitches hold the layers together. Nor does it mean a quilt whose filling was homemade batts of old recarded mattress cotton, wool from the family sheep, or cotton gleaned from the fields, or a multitude of pressed-work "string quilts" of odd-sized cotton scraps.

Rather, "plain" means straightforward pieced patterns organized around squares, rectangles and triangles. Quilts here were pieced of some scraps from the family's clothes sewing but these scraps were supplemented by large amounts of purchased fabric or composed solely of purchased fabric (Plates 22, 26, and 40). Only from the Depression period does one

Plate 18. Detail of quilt made by Mrs. Wellington Smith, Washington Township, Juniata County./Pieced print cottons in 3,072 triangles with print back. Back brought to front as edge treatment. 86″ × 77″ with 5-6 stitches per inch./Collection of the Juniata County Historical Society.

see quilts and tops composed exclusively (or close to that) of small scrap pieces (Plates 31 and 32). With some of the patterns promoted then, such as the *Double Wedding Ring* and *Grandmother's Flower Garden,* one could take particular advantage of the use of scraps.

"Plain" meant thoughtfully arranged and quilted blocks with careful sewing—usually around 7-8 stitches per inch on darker quilts, often 9, 10 or 11 on those with larger whole cloth expanses. Even on their thick comforts or haps, five evenly spaced stitches in straight rows were expected. Quilting patterns would vary in each of the top's sections: blocks, border(s) and sashing. In fact, a quilter's needlework and pieced corners were always examined first. Her overall design and color arrangements were judged second.

Similarly, the time spent in quiltmaking was not consumed in the making of small homemade batts which would be carefully alined on the quilt's back or lining as in Texas, New Mexico, and other parts of the South and Southwest. Such homemade batts were made in Pennsylvania, it appears, only prior to the availability of store-bought batting in the mid-nineteenth century. And although "plain" could mean string or pressed-work, as seen in area cotton or wool comforts of strip stars or Crazy blocks (Plates 101 and 36), the numbers of string quilts in the overall production are few when compared to what this author saw, for instance, in the state of New Mexico where they were the dominant quilt type.

Even the type and placement of the quilting frame reinforce what the quiltmakers and their extant old family quilts tell us—that Pennsylvania quiltmaking of the nineteenth and early twentieth centuries was generally done in conditions, though often rural and simple, not primitive or threadbare. Farm families here were relatively settled, well off financially and secure. Their large handmade footed quilting frames were set up all winter in the kitchen, parlor or spare bedroom (not suspended from the ceiling in a small room and rolled up when not in use as in the South) and they attest to Pennsylvania's relative affluence as does the wide use of purchased fabrics or quilting calicos, the fine unhurried and varied needlework, and the wide range of quilting motifs and pieced patterns (Plates 42-58).

Geraldine Johnson in her article "Plain and Fancy: The Socio-Economics of Blue Ridge Quilts" in *The Appalachian Journal* (Autumn 1982 pp. 12-35), after extensive fieldwork in the Appalachian areas of West Virginia, notes that "plain quiltmaking" there was distinctively different from the "plain" just described. She presents the thesis that for far too long quiltmaking elsewhere has been judged against the Pennsylvania model—both "plain" and "fancy"—and to the detriment of the truly plain and utilitarian seen by her in West Virginia (and by this author in New

Mexico). Pat Flynn Keyser in her article "Pieces and Patches" in *Quilt World* (April 1979, pp.4-7) discusses in detail this "plain" and popular rural Southern-style quilt. She includes drawings that illustrate the pressed-work method often used in making patches. She notes nonetheless that this string quilt of the South "... is usually mentioned [there] as an afterthought, almost apologetically, after [what are perceived as] the finer quilts of the house have been displayed. It is a type of quilt that can be put together in a very haphazard manner, [but] often a quilter will take the time to experiment with placement of color and evolve interesting designs."

Central Pennsylvanians also find it hard to show to others some of their plainer types, especially their heavy, often dark, comforts or haps. The condition of the pieces sometimes plays a part in their reluctance since many of their comforts were abused: relegated to the hunting cabin after home use had ended, stuffed into cracks as insulation, or used, as a writer for the *National Stockman and Farmer* advised in 1898 (August 18th, p. 519): "The truly economical woman gets all the wear possible out of everything. For example, she wears her gowns until frequent makings over have not left enough cloth for another renovation unless for a smaller person. After doing duty there she pieces them into comforts. When they grow shabby she either covers anew at the worn edges, or by putting two together makes a comfortable summer mattress for bed or cot. She never gives them to her husband for horse blankets with a certainty of their being torn to pieces in a week. One comfort folded into three thicknesses makes a very nice mat for a hammock, particularly one made of slats. On ironing day it saves the feet from aching by forming a soft place to stand on. When three persons are obliged to ride in a single carriage this same mat is rolled up and placed between the two occupying the seat, and the third person sits on the mat; thus all have comfortable seats."

These comforts or comfortables were made along with the often thinner "plain" quilts. Although some quiltmakers appeared to have avoided appliqué entirely, most made comforts either quilted or knotted together (called tied or tacked) at times. They appear in our earliest inventories and were advocated in national magazines and books on domesticity like Eliza Leslie's *House Book* (1846): "These are soft thick quilts used as substitutes for blankets, and laid under the bedspread. One of them is equal in warmth to three heavy blankets; and they are excellent in cold winters for persons who like to sleep extremely warm. In chambers with fire, or in a room that has had a fire all day, a comfortable will generally be found too warm a covering except in severe weather. It is best to use them in cold apartments only. If the house should be crowded with guests, so as to cause a scarcity of beds, a thick comfortable may be found a convenient

---

ESTATE INVENTORY OF
MAGERIT BIGGERS

Madison Township,
Columbia County
February 15th, 1819

To 1 Calico Bedquilt $2.00
To 2 Calico Frocks $4.00
To 1 Bedstead of Straw Tick
1 Fether Tick 1 Sheet 2 Blankets
1 quilt 1 coverlid 2 Pillows
and bolster $15.00

ESTATE INVENTORY OF
TOBIAS SHIRTZ

Limestone Township,
Montour County
August 7, 1821

one coverlead $10.00
one cotton quilt $2.00
one visted quilt $4.00

ESTATE INVENTORY OF
SARAH McENTIRE

Catawissa Township,
Columbia County
November 11, 1826

12 yds. sundry linsey
at 50 cts. per yd. $6.00
6 yards calico at 30 cts
per yd. 1.80
7 yds. Figured Bombasett
37½ 2.62½
4 yds. plain linen 33⅓ 1.33
1 Bed and bedding 10.00
1 Bed and blue cross-bar
coverlet 6.00
1 Tow and wool bird eye
coverlet 4.00
1 Linsey quilt 5.00
1 Dressed blanket 3.00
1 Calico quilt 4.50
1 stripped woolen quilt 4.00

---

substitute for a mattress." Forty-five years later *The National Stockman and Farmer* (October 8, 1891, p. 562) urged their readers to continue this tradition: "Did you ever make them? They are splendid—worth two calico comforts. In cutting rags for carpet I save all the good pieces out of cloth or jean coats or pants. I am very careful of all light clothes, as of course, most are black or dark ones. If any piece is too narrow I piece it on the machine and press out. I made my patch six inches square, to avoid so many seams; washed and ironed all out, then cut all patches by one pattern. I made 9 nine patches. I then took an old white blanket, colored it bright red and made a sash of it to join the patches. I made it six inches wide. Then with a strip of red or black at the top and bottom, makes you a large comfort. If preferred you can make the red in squares, and mix through to brighten. Now put in three pounds of cotton, line with something strong—say canton flannel—and quilt, not tack; and when it is twenty degrees below zero get under one and see if I am not right."

Predominantly called "haps" in certain areas of central Pennsylvania such as Huntingdon County, these, the thickest of quilts, were filled most often with wool. Their pieced tops might be made of a combination of fabrics or of all wool, cotton, old washed blankets, or even entirely of outing flannel as seen in a number of Perry County examples. Usually the wool haps were made of pressed-work blocks composed of random-size scraps (Plate 36) while cotton haps were almost always seen in traditional pieced patterns such as *Trip Around the World, Robbing Peter to Pay Paul,* or *Variable Star.*

"It was a five-comfort winter" said one Oklahoman to another, Dorothy Cozart, the quilt historian, two years ago. Comforts or haps—called britches, farm, camp, "soft" in the *Progressive Farmer,* "soogun" in parts of Texas and New Mexico—meant warmth and weight in the days before central heating. Charlotte Ekback, who now lives in Moorpark, California, but whose mother's side of the family came from Riddlesburg, Juniata County, remembers her uncle, Carleton Weyandt, remarking about "haps" to her as a small girl in 1948, "It is a wonder we did not grow up flat!" Remarks were made by this side of her family—of having their feet bent in or out because of the haps accumulated weight. Indeed, as a youngster with a hurt foot, they put Charlotte to bed, under a series of comforts and in order to keep their weight off her foot, they placed it in a five-pound coffee can. For those unaccustomed to sleeping under heavy bedcoverings, this might even sound cruel but indeed it was a good familiar feeling. As noted recently in correspondence to the author, John Hostetler, the eminent researcher and author on Pennsylvania's Amish said how an Amish nephew, upon having to sleep overnight in a hospital in Big Valley, Mifflin County, was un-

able to sleep without the comforting and familiar weight of his "haps."

These more mundane "plain" quilts held an important place in peoples' lives. The making of them, along with other family chores, was noted in a series of letters, written among members of a Perry County family. In May 1868, Eliza Reader remarked:

Dear uncle aunt and cousins

I Seat my self to drop you a few lines to let you know That i received your kind leters Wich found us all well and i hope this will find you all The same Butter is thirty cents Eggs fifteen Samuel A Smith Did not go with a girl we have our Corn and potatoes all planted We peased a quilt and quilted it We have our garden all made and some cabbage plants set out a readr plants are very scarce we got a leter from Rosey She landed safe She likes the west tretty Well hear is a patch of her dress Ellen Ebez hear is luther picture for you he said that you should get yours taken and give him yours hear i will give youns mine did youns hear any thing from aunt rous pleas let us know write soon

from your friend Eliza A Reader

Similar passing mention of quilts was made in other family letters:

. . . and we quilted too quilts from Diann and we had no place to make lye and Diann run the lye and then I took our lard over . . . (Mae Eby's letter from New Bloomfield on June 13, 1897); "i presume Manny and Sadie are so busy peacing quilts i will have to come over to help them what is wife Mary farman doing I suppose tending the calves (Lizzie C Turst's letter from Andersonburg on March 22, 1897).

A Perry countian, Virginia Wolf, wrote us recently with her remembrances of quilts and quiltmaking attitudes within her family. Her letter will in time, just as the others, attest to the importance of plain and fancy quilts in peoples' lives:

My grandmother, Mrs. Ida Troutman Sieber, [p. 36] made quilts for my mother, eight for my sister and eight for me as well as several comforters (then known as haps) for each of us. She started this work in 1905.

She loved to quilt and hand sew. She kept a frame up in her dining room which was very large Summer and Winter. This amused some people.

She used materials from her shirt waists (blouses to us); some were cotton and others, pure silk. She used my father's discarded suites and our coats—our dresses, etc.

The silk quilt is dated 1920.

The one comforter with the orange flowered lining was made in 1934 for me to take to College. It is probably the most used piece I have. My roommates and sorority friends loved to wrap in it or put it on the floor for a group to sit and study. Yes, we studied! The red and checked patches were coats of mine—a coat of mother's, my sister's and a suit of Dad's complete the creation.

My grandmother was born in 1881 in Pfoutz's Valley, Millerstown, R. D. 2 and lived there all her life.

My grandmother made all her clothes. She especially liked to

ESTATE INVENTORY OF EPHRAIM BONHAM

Washington Derry Twp., Columbia County November 22, 1828

One Bed consisting of one feather bed, one chaff bed, one bedstead, three blankets, four sheets, two bed quilts, two pillows, one bolster, 4 pillow cases . . . $20.00

ESTATE INVENTORY OF ANNE SHEDDEN

Liberty Township, Montour County September 24, 1829

1 White bed quilt with fringe.	$6.00
1 other quilt callico patchwork	2.50
1 " " " "	. . . . 1.75
1 " " " "	. . . . 2.25
2 " " " "	. . . . 3.00
1 " " " "	. . . 1.62½
3 Bed quilts woolen	. . . . 6.00
1 Double coverlet	. . . . 3.25
2 sheets & 10 pillow cases.	. . . . 4.00

ESTATE INVENTORY OF EZRA HARDER

Cattawissa Twp., Columbia County 1839

8 Quilts.	. . . . $20.00
1 Coverlet.	. . . . 4.00
2 Blankets.	. . . . 3.00
1 bed case.	50
3 Bolster cases	50
16 Sheets.	. . . . 10.00
26 Pillow cases.	. . . . 3.00
1 Comfortable.	25
1 piece of muslin for quilt lining	50
1 Quilt cover ready to quilt	. . 1.00
Ticking	. . . . 2.50

work with velvet and silks—taffeta was a choice fabric. You can see from the silk quilt she wore colors. Most of the materials were purchased in Newport and Harrisburg—some from Pittsburgh and even Atlantic City.

My grandmother died in 1950—89 years old and is buried in St. Michael's Cemetery, Pfoutz's Valley. This would be the site of the only church she ever attended.

Remembering the love and work which went in to these quilts and comforters, I carefully use them daily. You can see three of them in my living room, two in the dining room and the rest upstairs.

Crazy quilts and appliqués are generally what people considered their "fancy" pieces. On them was lavish needlework—often excessive by today's standards—multiple types of stitching and colors, even beads and sequins in the former, while the variety of motifs, closeness, evenness, and abundance of the quilter's running stitch were characteristic of the latter. As already noted, good needlework was expected on a Pennsylvanian's quilt whether they were working on a rudimentary *Nine Patch* or even a hap. But the needlework was supposed to be above average, very fine, on the fancy pieces—sometimes quilts reserved for the spare bed or "just for show" (Plates 8-11). Quite often it was imaginative and playful, repeating and inventing forms suggested by the applied patches (Plates 60-62). Rarely was it an overall pattern used throughout the piece as in waffle or fan quilting. (A number of very fine Perry and Cumberland county appliqués were done, however, in waffle quilting—Plates 47 and 64).

Fabric selection was also part of the criteria for a quilt to be labeled "fancy." Crazy quilts that were made of silk, velvets, and taffetas were considered "fancy" as contrasted to those Crazies made of wools, cottons, or outing flannel. Appliqués were made exclusively of store-bought fabrics and within a very narrow palette of solid colored or calicos of green and red on an all-white background and lining. Sometimes a third or fourth accent color was used, most often a yellow, yellow/orange or pink.

Appliquéd rather than pieced patterns were considered "fancy" although often a quilt such as *Blazing Star* might be considered as "special." Being a "special" quilt was different in peoples' minds from being "fancy." Family history and association as much as superior needlework, pattern or fabric types, made a quilt "special."

Within the area studied, certain appliqué patterns emerge as favorites as they were done repeatedly and in endless variations—sometimes in a naive manner. The *Whig Rose* or *Rose of Sharon* was by far the most often seen followed by—

ESTATE OF
ANNA LUNGER

Benton Township,
Columbia County
March 8, 1857

One bedsted & beding	11.00
1 Cover lid	3.00
1 new Calico quilt	1.50
1 woolin blanket	1.00
1 tow straw tick	.62
1 calico quilt old	.75
1 comforter	.25
1 peased quilt	.37

ESTATE OF
MATTHEW MCDOWELL

Scott Township, Columbia County
May 24, 1858

1 common Bedstead & Bedding	6.50
1 white & Black Bed Quilt	1.00
1 Bed Quilt (light col^d)	.50
1 " " (light col^d)	.87
1 French Bedstead	3.00

ESTATE OF
SAMUEL CREVELING

Fishing Creek Twp.,
Columbia County
May 14, 1859

one bedstid and tick	.50
one bedstid and beding	4.00
one bested and beding	
one shuttle work quilt	.75
one quilt block work	.50
one close work quilt	.50
one quilt nine patch	.50
one Coverlid showball	2.50
one Coverlid tater Blosum	4.50
one Coverlid Red	1.75
one Confortable	1.37½
one red and white Blanket	1.62½
one white Blanket	.50
one white Blanket	.62½
one Blue Blanket	.25

---

in descending order—the *Princess Feather, Tulip or Rose Wreaths, Cockscombs, Love Apples,* the *North Carolina Lily,* and *Laurel Leaves.* Notably absent as a dominant pattern in this eight-county region was the *Eagle* seen frequently in the Union/Snyder/Northumberland/Centre county region which was studied earlier (see pp. 13, 14 and 34 in *In the Heart of Pennsylvania,* Lewisburg, PA.: Oral Traditions Project, 1985).

The palette, applied designs, strong multiple border treatments, and needlework motifs of area appliqués remained consistent until we saw Dauphin County pieces where the fabrics' palette changed dramatically with the introduction of strong orange backgrounds as well as the switch to selectively used dark colored quilting thread (Plates 2-4). Medallion quilts, with applied or pieced work and in both very early and late examples, were another fairly strong tradition seen particularly in the Dauphin/Cumberland county area (Plates 8-12). (Well-designed and executed haps, on the other hand, became a rarity there.)

On the whole, appliqué patterns were bold abstractions of plants and flowers. Rarely was a rose, for instance, handled naturalistically, as it was in an appliqué made by an unknown Cumberland County quiltmaker (Plate 48). The trend to naturalize quiltmaking images occurred later in the 1920s and 1930s, both in terms of the palette which introduced pastels and in new designs like *Jonquils, Apple Blossoms,* and *Iris* (Plate 118).

For twelve decades in fact, area appliqués were done within a fairly prescribed formula, one which was lambasted by Ruth Findley in *Old Patchwork Quilts and the Women Who Made Them* in 1929: "Only a soul in desperate need of nervous outlet could have conceived and executed . . . the 'Full Blown Tulip,' a quilt of Pennsylvania-Dutch origin. It is a perfect accomplishment from a needlework standpoint yet hideous. The 'tulip' block is composed of eight arrow-shaped patches of purplish red; the eight petal-shaped patches inserted between the red arrows are a sickly lemon yellow. The center of each tulip is made of the material used for putting the blocks together—homespun of the most terrifying shade of brownish green, beyond question the accident of a private dyepot . . . the whole is surrounded by a second border . . . of dazzling bright orange. The green-red-lemon orange combination is enough to set a blind man's teeth on edge." How tastes have changed, for this is the palette sought after by today's collectors, one which all would agree is representative of most of the area's "fancy" quilts.

Plate 19. *Cumberland County hap. /*
Pieced print and calico cottons with
print back. Front brought to back as
edge treatment. 78″ × 82″ with 4
stitches per inch. / Collection of
Virginia Dougherty Goodyear.

Plate 20. *Quilt made by Margaret Ann Tyler Smith b. 1838 Lycoming County d. 1914 Wallis Run Lycoming County. / Pieced solid-colored and white cottons with print back. Applied solid-colored binding. 78" × 82" with 8-9 stitches per inch / Collection of Harriet Yaw.*

Nearly three thousand one inch red and white squares were cut in half by

Margaret Smith to form 5,636 triangles. She made this quilt for her son ca. 1900-1905. Its minute scale contrasts sharply to Sarah O'Neill's Double T (opposite).

Fig. 3. *Margaret Ann Tyler Smith with her granddaughter Rebecca Helen Smith.*

Plate 21. *Quilt pieced by Sarah Chilcoat O'Neill b. ca.1840 Cromwell Township, Huntingdon County, d. Rockhill Furnace, Huntingdon County and quilted by ladies of the Rockhill Church and Bertha Wilson Chilcoat b. 1884 Cromwell Township, Huntingdon County d. 1975 Huntingdon County. / Pieced solid-colored and white cottons with white back. Back brought to front as edge treatment. 78″ × 79″ with 4-5 stitches per inch. / Collection of Mrs. Frank Booher.*

Pieced blocks that were usually executed in 6″-8″ squares were sometimes done exceedingly large as were these 24″ examples. It was at the Perry County documentation day in particular that a sizeable number of quilts pieced on this large scale were recorded. This quilt was made for William McClain Chilcoat in 1886 and his initials are embroidered at the quilt's top edge.

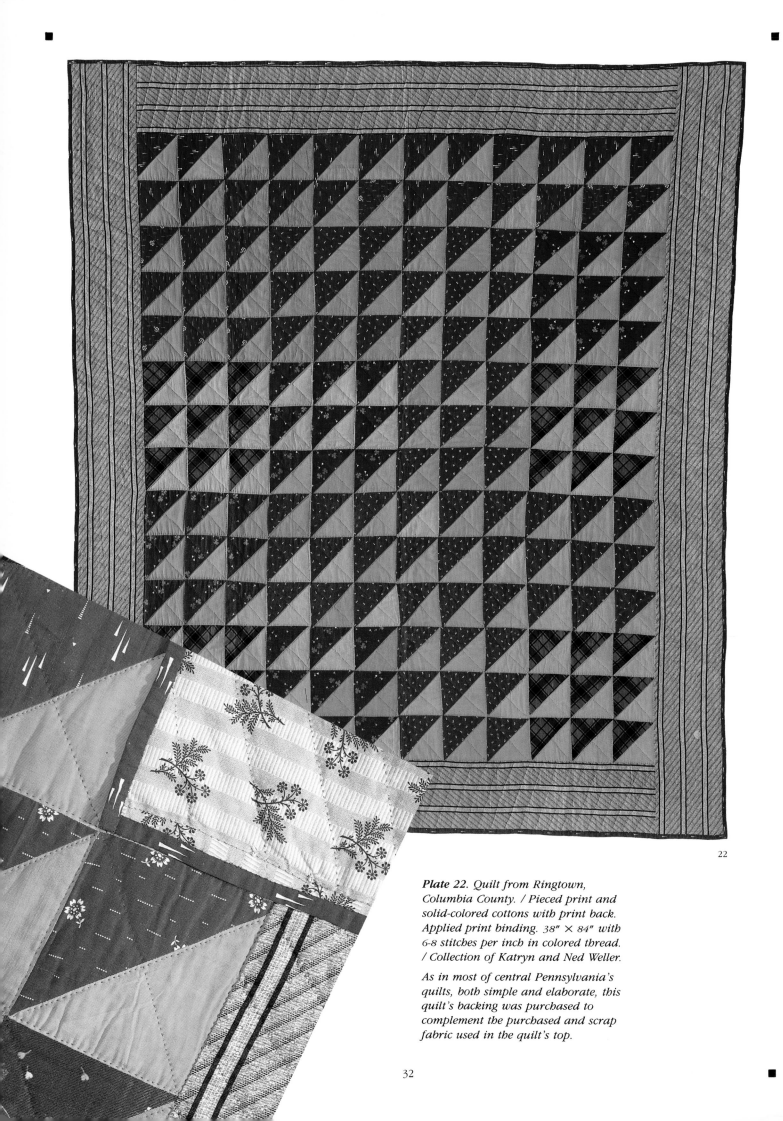

Plate 22. *Quilt from Ringtown, Columbia County. / Pieced print and solid-colored cottons with print back. Applied print binding. 38″ × 84″ with 6-8 stitches per inch in colored thread. / Collection of Katryn and Ned Weller.*

As in most of central Pennsylvania's quilts, both simple and elaborate, this quilt's backing was purchased to complement the purchased and scrap fabric used in the quilt's top.

Plate 23. *Detail of quilt made by Anna Mary Smith Macemore b. 1821 Three Springs, Huntingdon County d. 1895 Three Springs, Huntingdon County. / Pieced print and solid-colored cottons with print back. Front brought to back as an edge treatment. 70" square with 7 stitches per inch. / Collection of Emily M. Greenland.*

Some quilts just refuse to leave a family as in this example. Made by Anna Macemore sometime prior to her death in 1895 it was passed on to her son Lewis who gave it to his daughter Eliza Macemore Hoffman who in turn gave it to her daughter Lillian Hoffman Greenland. At Lillian's auction in 1985 it was bought back by family to be given to Emily Greenland, b. 1983, the original maker's great-great-great-grandaughter.

Plate 24. *Detail of quilt made by Adda Jane Ranck Zimmerman b. 1860 Mifflintown, Juniata County d. 1935 Mifflintown, Juniata County. / Pieced print and white cottons with white back. Applied print bindings. 64" × 74" with 8-10 stitches per inch. / Collection of Annette E. Lauver.*

24

Plates 25 and 26. *Quilts made by Annie or Jennie Bashore b. 1865 and 1867 McAlisterville, Juniata County d. 1900 and 1954 McAlisterville, Juniata County. / Pieced print, solid-colored, and calico cottons with print backs. Applied calico bindings. 81″ × 84″ with 8-9 stitches per inch and 74″ × 74″ with 11-12 stitches per inch. / Collection of Jane Bashore Marhefka and Nora Ella Bashore Singer.*

Figs. 4 and 5. *Jennie Bashore (far left) and Annie Bashore (left).*

26

35

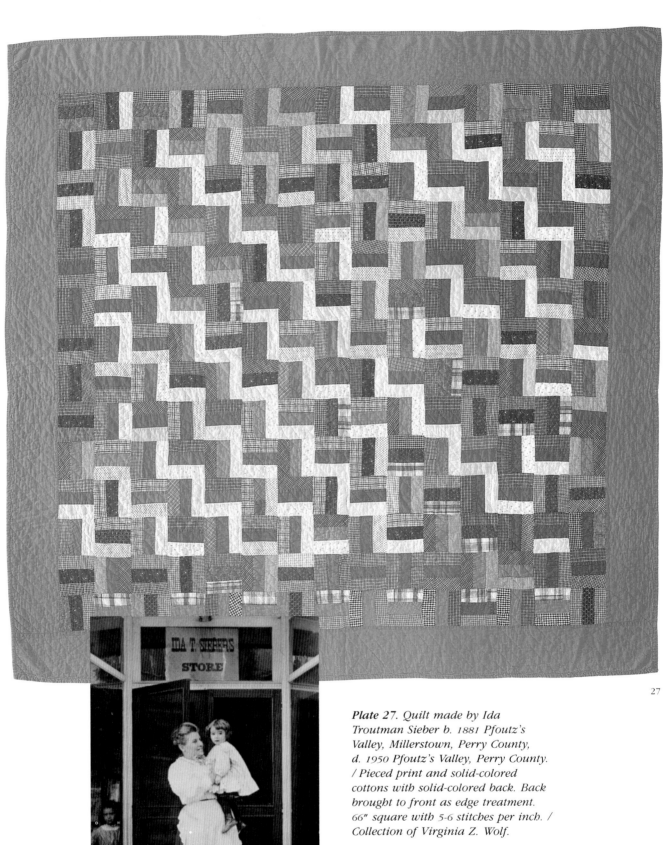

27

Plate 27. *Quilt made by Ida Troutman Sieber b. 1881 Pfoutz's Valley, Millerstown, Perry County, d. 1950 Pfoutz's Valley, Perry County. / Pieced print and solid-colored cottons with solid-colored back. Back brought to front as edge treatment. 66" square with 5-6 stitches per inch. / Collection of Virginia Z. Wolf.*

Starting in 1905, Grandmother Sieber began making quilts for Virginia, her sister, and their mother: 8 quilts for each as well as several haps. This Rail Fence typifies a well organized "plain" quilt. It was made from shirtwaist cotton remnants.

Fig. 6. *Ida Troutman Sieber holding Virginia Z. Wolf.*

Plate 28. *Detail of Columbia County quilt. / Pieced solid-colored and print cottons with print back. Back sewn to front as edge treatment. 77″ × 76″ with 4-6 stitches per inch. / Collection of Mary Margaret Reed.*

Plate 29. *Detail of quilt made by Nancy Beck Cox b. 1818 Spring Mount, Warriors Mark, Huntingdon County d. 1894 Antis Township, Blair County. / Pieced print and calico cottons with white back. Applied calico binding. 91″ × 76″ with 6-8 stitches per inch. / Collection of Donald and Margaret Baker Litzenberger.*

Plate 30. Columbia County crib quilt. / Pieced print and white cottons with print back. Back brought to front as edge treatment. 43″ × 42″ with 6-8 stitches per inch. / Collection of the Columbia County Historical Society.

Opposite page, top to bottom.

Fig. 7. Amanda Shellenberger (seated).

Plate 31. Quilt by Amanda Stuck Shellenberger b. 1868, Richfield, Juniata County d. 1936, Richfield, Juniata County. / Pieced print and solid-colored cottons with white back. Back brought to front as edge treatment. 82″ × 74″ with 10 stitches per inch. / Collection of Gladys Leitzel.

When Gladys Leitzel was setting up housekeeping in the 1930s her husband's grandmother made her this quilt. It is typical of quilts of that period in its use of many scraps, but unusual in its crazed border treatment.

Plate 32. Quilt made by Margaret Ida Loy Whitekettle b. 1875, Madison Township, Perry County, d. 1958 Newport, Perry County. / Pieced print and solid-colored cottons with white back. Applied solid-colored binding. 97½″ × 85½″ with 10-12 stitches per inch. / Collection of Pauline Whitekettle.

Mother and daughter, Margaret and Pauline Whitekettle, quilted this Postage Stamp *variation in 1933 having seen it first in the* Harrisburg Evening News. *It is a variation of the long-popular* Irish Chain.

Fig. 8. Margaret Ida Loy Whitekettle.

30

31

32

33

Plate 33. *Columbia County top. /
Pieced print, solid-colored, and calico
cottons. 66" × 75". / Collection of
Howard and Andrew Sechler.*

*One of only a few sampler tops or
quilts seen and it is the wildest.
Browns Goose appears to have been
a favorite of this quiltmaker's though
it rarely appears in other area quilts.
Her other pieced patterns were fairly
common ones.*

Plate 34. Quilt by Susie King Kay
b. 1858 Elkland Township, Sullivan
County d. 1922 Elkland Township,
Sullivan County. / Pieced silks with
print back. Front brought to back as
an edge treatment. 70" square. /
Collection of Ina Day Avery.

Fig. 9. Susie King Kay, her husband,
Albert, and their niece.

34

Plate 35. *Hap made by Margaret Frances Shaffer Summers, b. 1855 Mt. Pleasant Township, Columbia County d. 1949 Mt. Pleasant Township, Columbia County. / Pieced wools with outing flannel back. Front brought to back as edge treatment. 82" × 76" with 4 stitches per inch in colored thread and featherstitched on top. / Collection of Helen F. Roadarmel.*

Four pounds of cotton, yellow silkateen, and new wool fabric samples from the Danville Pants Factory were combined to make this understated but attractive comfort or hap. It was made in 1933 by Margaret Summers, a neighbor, for the present owner's wedding.

Fig. 10. *Margaret Frances Shaffer Summers*

Plate 36. *Hap made by Harriet Isabella Hoffman Frymire b. 1852 Delaware Township, Northumberland County d. 1930 Wallis Run, Lycoming County. / Pieced wools and outing flannels with fancy stitches in colored threads with solid-colored back. Applied solid-colored velvet binding. 51″ × 60″ with 6-7 stitches per inch. / Collection of Harriet Yaw.*

The greatest range and best organized wool Crazy quilts came from the more northern central Pennsylvania

counties. Of the more southern counties, only Perry had such heavy quilts or haps in any number. Some of Perry's were made out of more unusual fabrics—washed blankets and several times entirely made of outing flannel, a material usually reserved for a quilt's back. This dark wool Crazy was made just over the Sullivan County line, near Wallis Run.

Fig. 11. *Harriet Isabella Hoffman Frymire.*

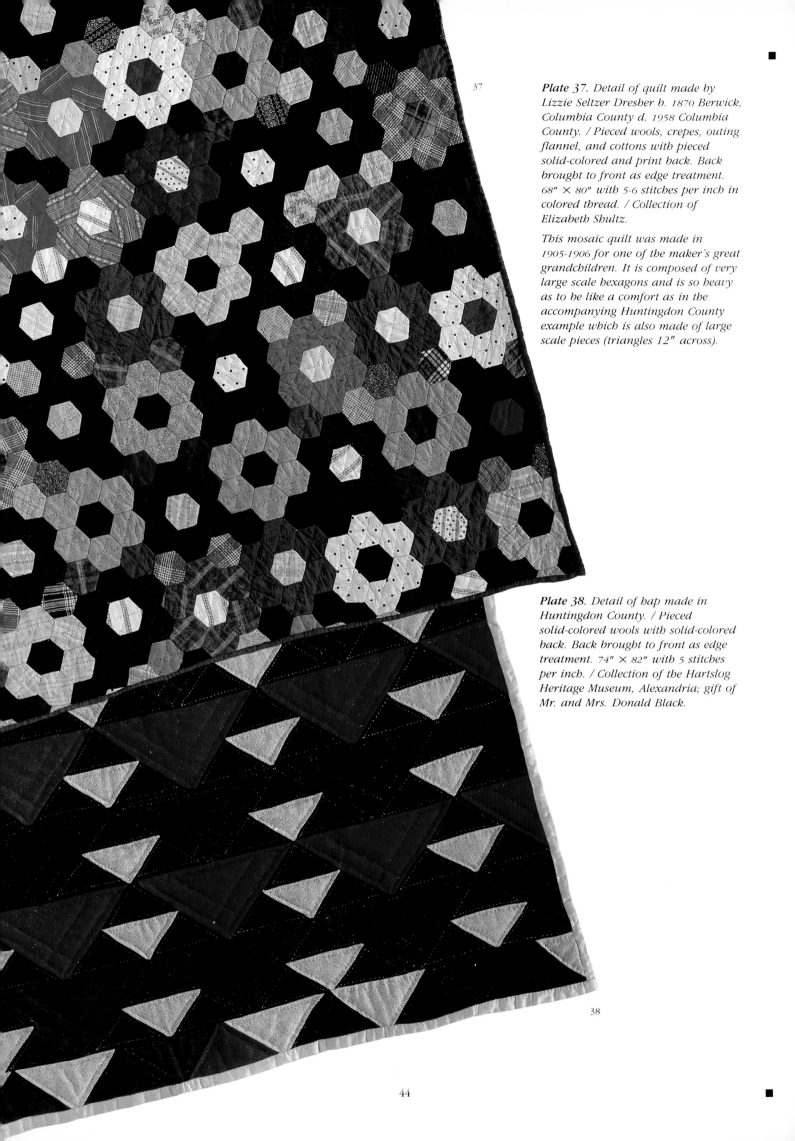

Plate 37. *Detail of quilt made by Lizzie Seltzer Dresher b. 1870 Berwick, Columbia County d. 1958 Columbia County. / Pieced wools, crepes, outing flannel, and cottons with pieced solid-colored and print back. Back brought to front as edge treatment. 68″ × 80″ with 5-6 stitches per inch in colored thread. / Collection of Elizabeth Shultz.*

This mosaic quilt was made in 1905-1906 for one of the maker's great grandchildren. It is composed of very large scale hexagons and is so heavy as to be like a comfort as in the accompanying Huntingdon County example which is also made of large scale pieces (triangles 12″ across).

Plate 38. *Detail of hap made in Huntingdon County. / Pieced solid-colored wools with solid-colored back. Back brought to front as edge treatment. 74″ × 82″ with 5 stitches per inch. / Collection of the Hartslog Heritage Museum, Alexandria; gift of Mr. and Mrs. Donald Black.*

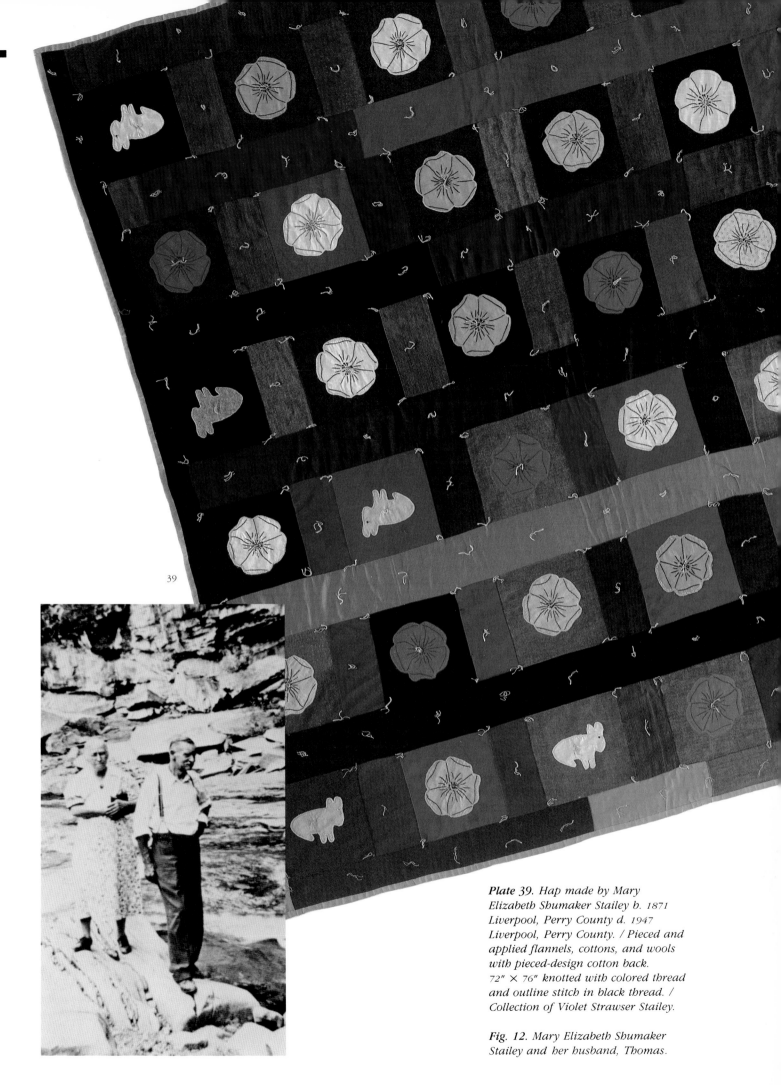

39

Plate 39. *Hap made by Mary Elizabeth Shumaker Stailey b. 1871 Liverpool, Perry County d. 1947 Liverpool, Perry County. / Pieced and applied flannels, cottons, and wools with pieced-design cotton back. 72" × 76" knotted with colored thread and outline stitch in black thread. / Collection of Violet Strawser Stailey.*

Fig. 12. *Mary Elizabeth Shumaker Stailey and her husband, Thomas.*

Plate 40. *Quilt pieced by Peninah Shaver Brown and quilted by Margaret Brown Clinger Longacre b. 1844 Mt. Union, Huntingdon County d. 1918 Germany Valley, Mt. Union, Huntingdon County. / Pieced calico cottons with white back. Applied calico binding. 71" square with 6 stitches per inch. / Collection of Virginia E. Robinson.*

Eight generations of women have been involved in some way with this Huntingdon County quilt which according to family tradition had its yellow calico purchased in 1846 by Mrs. Jane Shaver, mother of the piecer. Ocean Waves is a favorite area pattern done traditionally in calicos. When done in silks and velvets and embellished with fancy stitches and embroidered (opposite) the pattern can make the transition from "plain" to "fancy."

Plate 41. *Quilt made by Martha Jane Brandt Breckbill b. 1842, Monroe Township, Dauphin County, d. ca.1935, Boiling Springs, Dauphin County. / Pieced solid-colored wools, silks, and velvets with solid-colored chintz back. Back and front tucked in as edge treatment. 77" × 78" with*

fancy stitches in colored threads signed "HEB," "EBB," "MJB," and "RB." / Collection of Sarah Bricker Meixel Shultz.

Fig. 13. *Martha Jane Brandt Breckbill.*

42

Plates 42-44. *Quilt made by Agnes Magill Cummins b. 1825 McAlevy's Fort, Huntingdon County d. 1864 McAlevy's Fort, Huntingdon County. / Applied calico cottons on white top with white back. Applied calico binding. 99″ × 98″ with 8 stitches per inch. / Collection of Zettle's Antiques.*

Many of Huntingdon County's quilts were "washed to pieces," especially the relatively plain pieces. Quite the contrary here—a quilt in pristine condition with crisp mid-nineteenth century calicos appliquéd in as many as five layers. As with many of the area's appliqués, Agnes Cummins' quilt was kept "for show," to put out on a bed occasionally when a special guest was coming. The pattern is a very personal rendition of the familiar Oak Reel *and the* Princess Feather *but in the typical calico palette.*

43

44

Plates 45 and 46. Cumberland County quilt. / Applied calico cottons on white top with white back. Applied calico binding. 70¾" square with 9 stitches per inch. / Collection of Wilma Harlacher DeVanney.

46

Plate 47. Detail of quilt from Shughart family of Carlisle, Cumberland County. Probably made by Susan Shughart b. 1854 d. 1929. / Solid-colored cottons on white top with white back. Applied solid-colored binding 84" square with 7-9 stitches per inch. / Collection of Barbara W. Brown.

Many of the appliqué patterns popular elsewhere in the region were different in appearance when made in Cumberland County. As in these Cockscombs, the main fabric motifs are pierced to such an extent that the white behind them plays a very important role in the design. The pierced technique, rather like scherenschnitte, comes close to the appearance of reverse appliqué—only the quilt top's white field is used as a foil to the main cut fabric rather than inlaid colored fabrics.

47

48

Plate 48. *Detail of a Cumberland County quilt. / Applied print and calico cottons on white top with white back. Applied calico binding. 99" × 100" with 10 stitches per inch. / Collection of Wilma Harlacher DeVanney.*

Plate 49. *Detail of quilt made by Ella Lowe Foreman b. 1863 Carlisle, Cumberland County d. 1947 Carlisle, Cumberland County. / Applied solid-colored cottons on white top with white back. Applied calico binding. 86" square with 11-12 stitches per inch. / Collection of Marguerite Foreman Grove.*

Fig. 14. *Ella Lowe Foreman*

49

Plate 50. *Quilt made by Catherine Ann Thrasher b. 1847 Cherry Township, Sullivan County d. 1885 Cherry Township, Sullivan County. / Pieced and applied solid-colored cottons on white top with white back. Applied solid-colored binding. 85½" square with 5-6 stitches per inch in white and colored threads. / Collection of Phoebe Kelley.*

Catherine Thrasher, who had health problems and never married, spent much of her time doing handwork. Her pattern is not an uncommon one but the manner in which she has compressed the design is unusual as is its very stiff border.

Fig. 15. *Catherine Thrasher*

Plate 51. Quilt made by Margaret Miller b. 1798 Cumberland County d.1886 Cumberland County. / Applied print, solid-colored, and calico cottons on white top with white back. Applied calico binding. 96″ × 99″ with 9-8 stitches per inch. / Collection of Arlene Carns Wentzel.

According to family tradition, the pattern was taken from an old-fashioned table oil cloth. It is truly a one-of-a-kind appliqué and is composed of yet-crisp 1840s fabrics. Like many of this areas appliqués, it has a swag or vine border as contrasted to the more dominant use of sawtooth or vine borders further north in central Pennsylvania.

52

Plate 52. Quilt made by Isabella Jane
Shepley Rutter b. 1837 Halifax
Township, Dauphin County d. 1893
Halifax Township, Dauphin County. /
Applied solid-colored cottons on white
top with white back. Front brought to
back as edge treatment. 88″ square
with 8 stitches per inch, signed and
dated "I.J.S./March 9th/1857." /
Collection of Catherine S.
Zimmerman.

Plates 53-55. *Quilt made by Isabella Jane Shepley Rutter b. 1837 Halifax Township, Dauphin County d. 1893 Halifax Township, Dauphin County. / Applied solid-colored and calico cottons on white top with white back. Front brought to back as edge treatment. 89" × 90" with 8-9 stitches per inch, signed and dated "I.J.S./Feb. 8th 1858." / Collection of Catherine S. Zimmerman.*

Some families are the saving kind and Isabella's certainly was. Her

spinning wheel, samplers, portrait, daguerrotype, 1858 wedding dress as well as all the quilt patterns for three great dated appliqués are still owned by family. Isabella's paper patterns for her 1858 appliqué (opposite) have been reassembled. Pinpricks on the paper indicate areas where she meant to do inlaid appliqué work. The paper patterns were cut from penmanship exercises.

Fig. 16. *Isabella Jane Shepley Rutter*

54

55

Plate 56. *Detail of quilt made by Lydia Jacob b. 1820 Mifflin Township, Cumberland County d. 1893 Newville, Cumberland County. / Applied solid-colored and calico cottons on white top with white back. Applied white binding. 101" square with 9-10 stitches per inch. / Collection of Eleanor Lehman Bowman.*

Fig. 17. *Lydia Jacob*

56

Plates 57 and 58. *Quilt made by Mary Fraker Myers b. 1875 Cleversburg, Cumberland County d. 1964 Carlisle, Cumberland County. / Pieced and applied print, solid-colored, and calico cottons on white top with white back. Back brought to front as edge treatment. 86" square with 6-7 stitches per inch. Signed "Mary Myers." / Collection of Ella Killinger Pechart.*

Strong traditional appliqué could and was done late in the nineteenth and early in the twentieth century as in this Cumberland County quilt. The lattice treatment was used only once before in an area quilt.

57

Fig. 18. Mary Fraker Myers.

THINK
OF ME

Whether emblazoned in colored thread at the centermost part of the quilt "Pieced by Mother" as Hannah Norris Dean did on the quilt she made for her daughter, Eunice, (title page) or sewn inconspicuously in the white quilter's running stitch as Mary Guss did on her own Juniata County quilt, signatures played a large role in the making and in the giving of a wide variety of quilt types.

Among the earliest names and dates were those done in small counted cross-stitches. Juliann Lyons of Saville Township, Perry County made her appliquéd masterpiece with its cross-stitched signature at the age of twenty-one in 1855 prior to her marriage to Peter Smith (Plate 64). The placement of counted cross-stitch names, initials, and dates evolved from the marking of household textiles in the eighteenth and early nineteenth centuries. It is not seen here on quilts or tops made past 1865 and most often on pieces from 1840-1855.

Stamped or stenciled names are also seen mainly on mid-century bedcoverings but were sometimes on later pieces such as Anna F. Bashore's (Plate 67). Elaborately calligraphed signatures replete with flourishes and images—floral, biblical, vegetative—also were featured around the mid-century but were seen as late as the 1890s, though greater care in execution and detailing tended to be on the earlier examples. In contrast, simply inked signatures, or those executed in the quilter's running stitch were done over the entire time period studied. Those in white thread are easily overlooked because they are so subtle, often hidden amongst fine and abundant needlework. In contrast, the Crazy quilts' initials and names, are usually

prominent. If one does not find a centennial ribbon or other "dated" fabric in such quilts, one often finds either initials, dates or both (Plate 107), most from the 1880s. This trend continued even on the less flamboyant simple wool Crazies which were seen signed as late as 1935.

But it was not only on Crazy quilts that signing could be bold. Ellen Brown's appliquéd masterpiece conspicuously proclaimed in a colored chain stitch that the young lady completed it in "Forks Township, Sullivan County September 28, 1855 (Plates 60-62)," while the name of the recipient could not be missed on the appliqué made by his mother for Oren Landis in 1896 (Plate 66).

The names of not one but numerous friends (and often multiple makers) were stitched into or written on what are commonly called Signature or Friendship quilts, sometimes called Album quilts when a variety of pieced or appliquéd blocks were used as well. Such quilts were given at special times—often when one was leaving a community as when Reverend James H. Calder and his wife, Ellen Winebrenner, were to leave their church in Harrisburg and sail to China as missionaries (a quilt owned by the Smithsonian). Lest one forget—or to help them through more difficult times in unfamiliar, sometimes more primitive environments—such quilts served as positive reinforcements. Linda Lipsett sets the scene for many emotion-laden partings replete with their quilt gifts in *Remember Me* (San Francisco: Quilt Digest Press 1985) while Jessica Nicolls documents those made within the narrow geographic confines of the Delaware Valley in *Quilted for Friends* (Winterthur, Delaware: The Henry Francis DuPont Winterthur Museum, 1986).

One such friendship quilt was made for

Fig. 19. Anna Sechler Landis

Plate 59. *Detail of quilt top made by Anna Sechler Landis and her friends from Mt. Union, Huntingdon County and dated "April 15, 1895/Mt. Union/Pa." Pieced silks and velvets with fancy stitches in colored threads with beads, sequins, and painted images. 62″ square./Collection of LaRue L. Obler. In addition to the many names in the quilt's central motif there are squares embroidered with "Scotland," "Rhode Island," "Ohio," "Bessie Stratford," and "94." Many more quilts with names and dates were seen in this current documentation effort than in the previous study.*

Mary M. Coe by friends she was leaving behind in the New Kingstown area of Cumberland County in the late 1840s. Inside each of the quilt's forty-two red and white pieced *Union Square* blocks were inscriptions similar to those one might expect to have seen written in an autograph album of the period:

When this you see remember me/and bear in mind/A trusty friend is hard to find/ Margaret Mutch/July 29, 1847.

The world can never give/The bliss for which we strive/For not the whole life to love/Is all of death to die./Mary A. Law

For Christians here to part/Is affecting to the heart/But again in heaven to meet/Is pleasing consolatory and sweet/Jacob S. Hoster

How sweet the strong untiring love/That makes us both to part/And though we may far off remove/We shall be joined in heart/ Elizabeth Fought

When I am dead and in my/grave and all my bones are/rotten then look at this and/think of me lest I be forgotten/Elizabeth Mutch

Kingstown March/27 A 1848/May our hearts affections move,/To the home our spirits love:/To the seats prepared above,/And our Savior's blessings prove/Aliza I. Williams

Though young and fair thou yet will find/ This life a thorney way/Then set thy heart and move thy mind/I meet its saddest day/ Catharine Fought/April 12, 1848

Margaret Dill to her friend/Mary M. Coe/ And when our end/of life shall be/May we ascent to/Dwell with thee in heaven/1847

When we asunder part/It gives us inward pain/But we shall still be joined in heart/ And hope to meet again. Eve Dill.

Whilst memory points thee to/friends more dear O grant my/request I ask only this Bestow/one kind thought on the friend/that wrote this/Sarah A. Williams/June 12, 1848

However, some of the penned inscriptions were unmistakably composed with a quilt in mind:

When on your bed this you see/Then remember that we together/oft have been/And at one alter prayed/Oh how sweet the moments/Passed away/Margaret Kosher

Mary M. Coe/My kind friend so dear/ May this patch of love your heart/Oft cheer as oft you under/it your eyes do close/ May have a happy and sweet repose/ Peter Barnhart

Mary M. Coe/When you are absent and gone/ And trouble and trials of heart/Do come may this patch that/I present to you in love/Raise your drooping heart to/Christ above/Mary Barnhart

Mary M. Coe/My esteemed friend/To you this patch do send/That it may help your album/quilt to close/And you under it may have a/sweet repose/Elizabeth Peterman

Sentiment, albeit it shorter, was expressed on the Album

ESTATE INVENTORY OF
JAMES MOORE

Huntingdon County 1803

Six Single Blankets 12.00
One pair of fulled Blankets . . 4.00
Three Coarse Bed quilts 4.00
One old Blanket 1.00
one Stuff Bedquilt 4.00
Two Callico Bedquilts 4.00
one Single   ditto 2.00
one Coverlid Maple Bedsted . . 4.00

ESTATE INVENTORY OF
THOMAS KYLER

Huntingdon County
September 20th 1824

4 Woolen Quilts @ 3.00 each . 12.00

ESTATE INVENTORY OF
GIDEON BYERS

Tyrone Township,
Huntingdon County
November 12th, 1832

one cradle quilt and boulster . 2.00
one bed quilt 25
one blanket 1.00
one calico quilt 3.00
one do happ 4.00
one light colored coverlid 2.00
one Marseilles quilt 5.00
one blue and white striped
    calico quilt 4.00

ESTATE INVENTORY OF
RACHEL BLAIR

Dublin Township,
Huntingdon County
July 7th 1839

Seven flannel quilts at
    fifty cents each 3.50
two old calico quilts at
    twenty five cents each 50
one feather bed w/underbed
    w/pillow & quilts 7.00
one other feather bed w/slats
    quilts boster & pillows 10.00

quilt made for Matilda and Samuel A. Worman of Espy, Columbia County (Plate 63):

Mary Ann Jacoby/Berwick/Never Forget

There is a place where parted friends/meet again—will you/meet me there/H./Berwick

Catharine Bowman/A place in your memory I ask

Elmira E. Davis/Spruce Grove/'Will you remember'

Dorothy Ann Bowman/Mifflinville/Think of me—

A reminescence of Respect and Esteem/from Matilda's friends/Berwick 185–.

These are sentiments, which express the needs and concerns both of those being left behind as well as for those going to parts unfamiliar.

Signature quilts were of all types: appliqués that reflected the variety and complexity of patterns within a group's repertoire (Plate 63) as well as simple but bold *Rolling Stones,* numerous *Album* or *Chimney Sweep* patterns, and *Baskets, Bear Paws, Flying Geese,* in addition to Crazy and Log Cabin-styles. Of the three Friendship quilts owned by the Cumberland County Historical Society, two were pieced star patterns: one made for a teacher, Agnes Myers, at the Dickinson Public School in the fall of 1898 by "55 Little Children" and the other made by Harriet Sheaffer Duler and four of her friends.

The greatest number of signatures are seen on the local fundraisers where each name meant the collection of a sum of money—from five cents to five dollars— for each name on the quilt. Bets Ramsey of Tennessee discovered a Perry County quilt which had the names of twins stitched between *Wheel Spokes,* a favorite pattern for fundraisers, and much like another made in neighboring Juniata County. The latter example was organized by Class #9 of the Port Royal Methodist Sunday School prior to October 1929 when it was completed. Each class member—and there are hundreds represented—paid ten cents to be included in the salute to their teacher and superintendent of Juniata County Schools, Professor S. W. McClure. Upon completion the quilt raised additional funds for the church when it was purchased by Jonas Fogelman for his wife Cora's birthday. It has since been given to their son, the present owner.

Fundraisers most often are white whole cloth quilts with the donors' names, the recipient's, and/or any place names or dates embroidered in the very washable and enduring Turkey red thread. Often they have made their way from the family who initially was given or purchased them to an historical society of the area. This was the case of the one currently owned by the Hartslog Heritage Museum in Alexandria, Huntingdon County. It was organized by the Junior Epworth League No. 4931 of nearby Petersburg and completed in 1918. Many of its varied blocks include the amount actually raised by each cluster of names. Its palette of red embroidery on whole white cloth is often rendered in pieced designs as in two red and white examples owned by the Huntingdon County Historical Society. One is an *Expanded Nine Patch* and the other a cross design (Plate 72).

Documentation of these fundraising quilts can often go beyond the recording of the inscribed names. For example, the Ladies Home Missionary Society of the Silver Spring Presbyterian Church in Mechanicsburg, Cumberland County, completed their fundraiser on December 12, 1883. The ladies made the simple red and white pieced quilt (Plate 73) by collecting ten cents for every name and gave it to Reverend T. J. Ferguson who later gave it to his daughter on the West Coast from where it was returned to the church in the 1960s. The Ladies Home Missionary Society's quilt is now at the church along with the minute book which recorded that $20.30 was raised by the quilt by August 25, 1883.

Another local fundraiser, currently owned by William Hileman, was made in 1917 by the Ladies Aid Society of Eyer's Grove Methodist Church in Columbia County (Plate 69). The present owner's father bought the quilt for ten dollars when it was auctioned and his wife complained about it for years being very put out that he had spent such money on a quilt she had sewn!

While most fundraisers were in this dominant palette as either outline embroidered or simple pieced cotton patterns, multicolored examples have been found as a Log Cabin, as a tied hap of suiting samples, and as a Crazy quilt in velvets. The latter is an exuberant display of fabric types as well as needlework stitches and was made by Salem Ladies Aid Society of the Salem E.U.B. Church in Blairs Mills, Juniata County between 1931 and 1932 (Plate 71). The single area Log Cabin fundraiser (Plate 70), was described in a period newspaper article titled, "A Handsome Quilt." It stated that The Ladies Aid Society of the Pine Grove Presbyterian Church, Dublin Township, had just completed their silk quilt, "It contains twenty-five patches, with twelve hundred names of persons who contributed from ten cents to six dollars to a name, making a total of $337.00. The solicitors are as follows: Mrs. Bruce Appleby–$55.10, Miss Rhoda & Cora Peterson–$38.00, Miss Cora Stitt–$36.00, Mrs. Chas. & Nevin

ESTATE INVENTORY OF
JOHN LOGAN

Huntingdon County
August 19th 1840

7 comforts	*14.00*
1 calico quilt, yellow border . .	*8.00*
1 " " , blue do	*7.00*
2 coverlids double diaper (old)	*6.00*
1 (old) calico quilt	*2.50*
10 white blankets	

ESTATE INVENTORY OF
BENJAMIN NEARHOOF

Warriors Mark Twp.,
Huntingdon County
1853

1 set quilting frames	*.25*

ESTATE INVENTORY OF
ISABELLA B. STITT

Dublin Twp., Huntingdon County
1857

1 Feather Cover	*2.00*
1 Callico quilt blue	*3.00*
1 Do red patch	*2.00*
1 Old quilt close quilted	*1.00*
2 Sheets	*1.00*
4 old flanell quilts .50	*2.00*
1 Coverlid	*5.00*
1 Do old	*2.00*

ESTATE INVENTORY OF
RACHEL SHUGART

Warriors Mark,
Huntingdon County
1867

7 quilts	*14.00*
6 comforts	*14.00*
3 Blankets	*12.00*
2 Cradle Comforts	*.25*

Robison–$30.00, Miss Louisa Wilson–$26.00, Mrs. John Swan–$25.00, Miss Myra Peterson–$21.35, Miss Edna Harper–$17.00, Mrs. W. C. Swan–$12.00, Miss Minnie Hart–$11.50, Miss Mary Peterson–$10.00, Miss Vivian Appleby–$8.55, Miss Anna Doran–$8.00, Miss Mary Harper–$5.45, Miss Maude Stitt–$5.50, Mrs. W. H. Swan–$5.00, Mrs. Mary Jones–$5.00, Miss Lizzie Stitt–$4.35, Mrs. J. J. Swan–$3.00, Miss Mattie Swan–$2.45. The proceeds of the quilt is to be applied to furnishing the interior of the new church, the quilts will be offered for sale in the near future. The Society wishes to thank all who aided in this work. The new church will be dedicated soon." Mrs. Bruce Appleby's own collection list itemized both her square's donors and the amounts they gave—which ranged from 25¢ to $5.10. Her solicitations totaled $55.10 or $17.10 more than Rhoda and Cora Peterson's square! Mr. Appleby, her husband, then bought the quilt for $10.50 when it was put up for sale. Today, the quilt, the "list of names on my church quilt patch," the newspaper article as well as the list of all those soliciting and their signature totals is in the possession of Mrs. Appleby's grandchild.

With all these quilts cited along with others not mentioned, one would think that signatures were commonplace on quilts but these were exceptions rather than the rule. Although signing quilts played an important role in the identification of makers and recipients, and in female, neighborhood, and church bonding—especially in fundraising projects—such quilts are relatively rare. Not counting Crazy quilts, only about two percent of all those quilts seen were signed.

In the absence of actual signatures, there are those family quilts which reflect a particular woman's work—noted for their exceptionally fine needlework, for a consistently imaginative handling of simple pieced patterns, or for strong eccentricities. Also, there are those with their attached notes or stories such as one owned by the State Museum in Harrisburg, (#31.96.18): "The patchwork was made by Sally Albright in West Hanover Twp., Dauphin, Pa. Sally was an invalid and when her sister came home with her pay, Sally begged a little money and secretly purchased the calico. When the quilt was finished she gave it to her sister. The quilting done by Mrs. Moyer who was called 'Quilt Moyer' on account of her expert quilting." Most families

know who made or received their quilts not because of signatures but rather, because of their family's oral traditions about people like "Quilt Moyer." They in turn pass these stories onto others like ourselves, so that we never forget.

Plates 60-62. *Quilt made by Ellen Brown b. 1832 Forks Township, Sullivan County d. 1915 Muncy, Lycoming County. / Pieced and applied print and calico cottons on white top with white back. Applied calico binding. Signed "Forks Township Sullivan County / September 28, 1855." 86" × 74" with 11-13 stitches in white and colored thread. / Collection of Etta E. Shoemaker.*

Over two hundred hearts, two weeping willow trees, and "Forks Township Sullivan County/September 28, 1855'"(written in large chain-stitched script) allude to a story now lost about the young woman who made this remarkable quilt. Swirling swastikas, spoked wheels, Lemoyne stars, and diamonds are all double-row quilted. Hundreds of quilted leaves spring forth from and add interest to the exceptionally large appliquéd plant—a tree of life in a sunflower-type pattern. Thousands of green stitches etch the veins into the green calico of the stems and leaves. Also unusual is the depiciton of daffodils. Ellen Brown never married and eventually left Forks Township to live with her sister in Muncy, Lycoming County about thirty miles away. Relatives submitted her quilt to the Chicago Evening American's *quilt contest in* 1929 *where it was a finalist.*

60

61

62

Plate 63. *Quilt made by the friends of Martha Matilda Stiles Worman and Samuel A. Worman of Espy, Columbia County between 1851-1854. / Pieced and applied solid-colored and calico cottons on white top with white back. Front brought to back as edge treatment. 94" × 84" with 9-10 stitches per inch. / Collection of Howard and Andrew Sechler.*

This Friendship Album *quilt of thirty different squares was made as "A reminiscence of Respect and Esteem/from Matilda's friends /* Berwick 1851." *Each square was made by a different individual and while the blocks' execution range from refined to moderately crude, the top is finely quilted with typical period quilting motifs including the pineapple of hospitality. "M. Matilda Worman / Samuel A. Worman / Espy / (Wednesday evening 11¾ O. Clock) January 4th 1854" completes the inscription in one of the blocks. What is alluded to is now lost but most likely was when the job was completed unless they married late in life, as Samuel was born in 1818.*

63

64

65

Plates 64 and 65. *Quilt made by Juliann Lyons Smith b. 1834 Saville Township, Perry County d. 1913 Saville Township, Perry County. / Applied solid-colored cottons on white top with white back. Applied binding. 100" × 101" with 10-11 stitches per inch. / Collection of Charlotte Sweger.*

Fig. 20. *Juliann Lyons Smith with her husband, Peter Smith.*

66

Plate 66. *Quilt made by Mary Elizabeth Webber, b. Boiling Springs, Cumberland County d. South Middleton Township, Cumberland County. / Pieced and applied solid-colored and print cottons with print back and some padded work. Applied solid-colored binding. 78" square with 6-7 stitches per inch. Signed and dated "OREN LANDIS 1896." / Collection of Ruth Snyder.*

67

Plate 67. Detail of quilt made by Anna Bashore b. 1865 McAlisterville, Juniata County d. 1900 McAlisterville, Juniata County. / Pieced print and solid-colored cottons with apron gingham back. Applied calico binding. 80″ × 83″ with 12-13 stitches per inch. / Collection of Jane Bashore Marhefka.

Fig. 21. Mid-nineteenth century tools for stamping and stencilling names such as those seen on the tops and backs of some area quilts as well as on labels attached to them as in Anna Bashore's example above. / Collection of the Chester County Historical Society. Photo: courtesy The Henry Francis Du Pont Winterthur Museum.

68

Plate 68. Detail of quilt made for Elisabeth Hartsler, a minister's wife near Belleville, Mifflin County ca. 1860. / Applied print and solid-colored cottons on white top with white back. Applied print cotton binding. 84″ square with 10-11 stitches per inch. Signed in counted cross stitch "Elisabeth Wife of Rev. J. Hartsler." / Collection of Laetena Shelley.

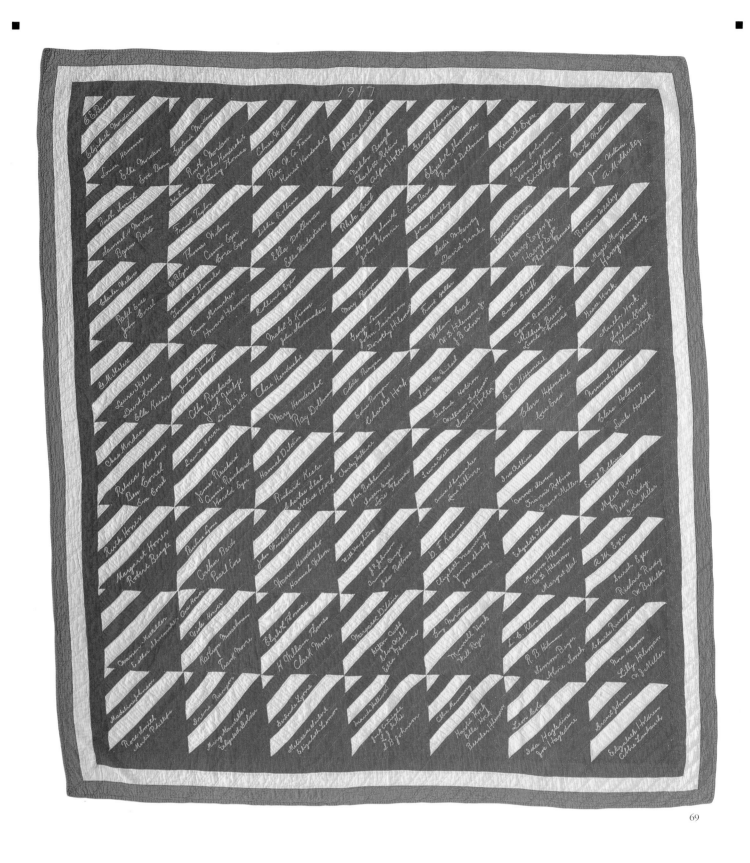

Plate 69. *Quilt made by the Ladies Aid Society of Eyer's Grove Methodist Church dated "1917." / Pieced solid-colored and white cottons with white back. Applied solid-colored binding. 72" × 82" with 6-9 stitches per inch. / Collection of William Hileman.*

Plate 70. *Detail of quilt made by the Ladies Aid Society of the Pine Grove Presbyterian Church, Pine Grove, Huntingdon County in 1902. / Pieced print and solid-colored silks and velvets with solid-colored silk back. Applied ruffle. 63" × 64" and tied in colored thread / Collection of Margaret Appleby Kemmler.*

Plate 71. *Detail of quilt made by the Salem Ladies Aid Society, Blair Mills, Juniata County. Signed and dated "1931/1932." / Pieced velvets with chintz back. Front brought to back as edge treatment. 75" × 72" with fancy stitches in colored threads. / Collection of Rosie Goss.*

Figs. 22 and 23. *The Salem Church and some of the Salem Ladies Aid Society.*

70

71

72

Plate 72. Huntingdon County quilt finished November 11, 1937 and pieced earlier. / Pieced solid-colored and white cottons with white back. Back brought to front as edge treatment. 69" × 92" with 7 stitches per inch. / Collection of Huntingdon County Historical Society.

Plate 73. Quilt made by the Ladies of the Silver Spring Missionary Society, Silver Spring, Cumberland County and dated "1883." / Pieced solid-colored and white cottons with white back. Back to front as edge treatment. 88" × 84." / Collection of the Silver Spring Presbyterian Church.

STARS FOREVER

Other than the *Nine Patch* and the *Double Nine,* no pattern was seen more often than stars of all sizes, construction types, fabrics, and colors. In this project the earliest was a very worn, very large but still documentable late-eighteenth century *Central Medallion Star* made by a Huntingdon County woman and owned by the county's historical society. It was one of four *Central Medallion Stars* seen, the others being smaller quilts such as those made by a member of the Enck family of Carlisle, Cumberland County in the 1840s.

For more than one hundred-fifty years, the star which appeared most often was the *Variable Star* which is composed of a single large square and eight triangular points. It was followed in popularity by the *LeMoyne Star, Bethlehem Star* or *Lone Star* and lastly the *Broken Star,* all composed of diamonds. The *Variable Star* pattern was seen in 1830s chintz fabrics as well as one hundred years later in the last throes of the calico rage (Plate 82). They were most often pieced in blocks averaging five to seven inches square but occasionally were made smaller. Either scrap or purchased fabrics could be used alone in any *Variable Star* but often they were combined for maximum effect. Sometimes a series of smaller triangles were pieced onto the eight points of the *Variable Star* creating, as in Margaret Steel Entrekin's quilt, the *Feathered Star* (Plate 77). With few exceptions, those *Feathered Stars* seen within the entire fifteen-county area now surveyed are of the earliest vintage.

Another quilt by this young Huntingdon County woman combines the single dominant *Bethlehem Star* with a galaxy of *Variable Stars* all executed in 1830s fabrics (Plate 75). Later her only son, William, had his name stenciled on the back of all of his mother's quilts (she had married in 1833 then died in 1840) in an effort, according to family tradition, to ensure his ownership after his father's second marriage.

It is this single large star, composed often of seven hundred diamonds, that is the favorite quilt of area families today. As a consequence, nineteenth- and early twentieth-century examples that come out at auction command high prices. Many were saved and as the nineteenth century progressed their scale increased from that of Margaret Entrekin's until it spread across the top's entire surface as a late example by a Sullivan County woman (Plate 83).

In the 1920s McCall's introduced a new pattern called the *Broken Star* and it became, as had its predecessor, the *Bethlehem Star,* a favorite. Minnie Mowery Hudleson's is a fine ex-ample, one of many seen (Plate 117). Her quilts were first made out of necessity, later "just for nice"—as a hobby along with her five-strand braided rugs. The bulk of her extant quilts emphasizes the pastel palette of the 1930s whether they are traditional pieced patterns or the newly introduced appliqués.

The many star variations we saw evolved as variations of these half dozen types: *Variable, Feathered, LeMoyne, Bethlehem, Broken,* and strip stars. They did not approach, however, the 104 variations that Philip Curtis mentioned in *American Quilts* (Newark, New Jersey: Newark Museum, 1973). Nonetheless, they were, as he noted, the most popular single image, reserved not just for pieced work but also occasionally appliquéd in a single piece of fabric, and used as quilting pattern as well.

Another popular star quilt but of quite different construction was the strip or string star of pressed-work in cottons, wools, or silks. Such stars emphasized small scrap pieces, each piece sewn on a diamond-shaped foundation, either in uniform strips of fabric or of very random pieces. The diamonds were then pieced together (a fine example is illustrated in the author's article on central Pennsylvania's quilts in *Antiques,* January 1987). They emerge as an important and prevalent star type after the Civil War, at a time when the pressed-work Log Cabin was also popular. They were often made in crepes and wools and as late as the 1930s. Those cotton examples usually had fabrics dating from the 1920s and 1930s. Most often tops of these stars were worked up as comforts or haps.

Like its cousin the *Bethlehem Star,* the *LeMoyne Star* composed of eight diamonds, was popular over the entire period surveyed. They are featured in the border of a Juniata County quilt of the second half of the nineteenth century (Plate 79), a quilt that features those fabrics most often seen in area pieced quilts—the pink and green quilting calicos. Quilting calicos were found by Nancy Roan (a quilt historian from the Goshenhoppen region of Montgomery County, who remembers her mother mentioning them) as being distinct from dress calico in that they were cheaper fabrics which did not retain their color or wear as well. Nancy also found them mentioned in an area store ledger (the Hildegrass and Stetler Store of Pennsburg, Montgomery County) in 1848. John Gehman of Butter Valley bought some of these quilting calicos for twelve cents a yard in 1833.

Plate 74. Detail of a Dauphin County quilt./Pieced print cottons with white back. Front brought to back as edge treatment. 80" × 90" with 5-6 stitches per inch./Collection of Patricia Meyers.

Plate 75. *Quilt made by Margaret Steel Entrekin b. 1809 Huntingdon, Huntingdon County d. 1840 Huntingdon, Huntingdon County. / Pieced print cottons on white top with white back. Applied print cotton binding. 106" square with 7-10 stitches per inch. / Collection of Mr. and Mrs. William E. Cremer.*

Like other of our area's quilts—also all made with star motifs—this one is typically large and a size not seen again for nearly a century. This star, as well as another by Margaret Steel (Plate 77), was made near the time of her marriage to James Entrekin in 1833. She was dead seven years later.

Plate 76. Dauphin County quilt. /
Pieced print and calico cottons on
white top with white back. Back
brought to front as edge treatment.
84" × 86½" with 8-10 stitches per
inch. / Collection of Wilma Harlacher
DeVanney.

77

Plate 77. *Details of quilt made by Margaret Steel Entrekin b. 1809 Huntingdon, Huntingdon County d. 1840 Huntingdon, Huntingdon County. / Pieced print cottons on white top with white back. Applied solid-colored binding. 96″ × 80″ with 7 stitches per inch. / Collection of Mr. and Mrs. William E. Cremer.*

Plate 78. *Quilt made by Mary Elizabeth Webber or Mrs. David Landis, Boiling Springs, Cumberland County. / Pieced and applied print and solid-colored cottons with pieced designed back. Back brought to front as edge treatment. 78" square with 8 stitches per inch. / Collection of Lyndall Gerhardt.*

Three quilts from the Landis family of Boiling Springs were brought to three

different documentation days. Each one was very special in execution and eccentric in design (Plate 66). This quilt is also one of only several seen with a pieced-back design. Its Orange Peel pattern was done in the second largest scale (22" square) seen for a traditional pieced block, one which was usually done as a 6" patch.

Plates 79 and 80. *Quilt, with detail at right, made by Adda Jane Ranck Zimmerman b. 1860 Mifflintown, Juniata County d. 1935 Mifflintown, Juniata County. / Pieced print and calico cottons with white back. Applied calico binding. 82" × 80" with 9 stitches per inch and signed in colored thread "Adda J. Zimmerman." / Collection of Annette E. Lauver.*

Swirling swastikas or "hexfeiss," as the Pennsylvania Germans called them, are quilted in the fill-in blocks in this star quilt. Its pink and green calicos were popular in many areas of Pennsylvania. In the seven counties surveyed this time, it was a color combination not seen in as overwhelming numbers as in the previous study.

80

81

Plate 81. *Detail of Cumberland County quilt. / Pieced calico cottons with white back. Front brought to back as edge treatment. 80" × 99" with 8 stitches per inch. / Collection of Wilma Harlacher DeVanney.*

Plate 82. Quilt made by Mary Fraker
Myers b. 1875 Cloversburg,
Cumberland County d. 1964 Carlisle,
Cumberland County. / Pieced print,
solid-colored, and calico cottons with
white back. Back brought to front as
an edge treatment. 80" square with
8-9 stitches per inch. / Collection of
Ella Killinger Pechart.

Plate 83. *Quilt made by Ella May*
Magargel Sheets b. 1865 Lairdsville,
Lycoming County d. 1933 Hills Grove,
Sullivan County. / Pieced and applied
solid-colored, print, and calico cottons
with solid-colored back. Applied

solid-colored binding. 53" × 67" with
6 stitches per inch. / Collection of
Carol Magargel St. Clair.

Fig. 24. *Ella May Magargel Sheets,*
far right.

In Fashion

Two new quilt types were introduced nationwide in the second half of the nineteenth century—Log Cabin variations called Canadian patchwork in S.F.A. Caulfield and Blanche C. Saward's *The Dictionary of Needlework, An Encyclopedia of Artistic, Plain and Fancy Needlework* (London: L. Upcott Gill, 1882) and Crazy quilts or the "Japanese type" as they were categorized at local fairs. Both were extremely popular with women in central Pennsylvania when they were first introduced and they continued to be made here, though in more limited numbers, well past the turn of the century.

Both Log Cabins and Crazy quilts were initially executed as strip pressed-work—fabrics sewn to a foundation without any of the sewing construction visible on their tops. Both utilized small strips of fabric of a wider variety than seen in the average pieced work quilt of the period. The Crazy pushed that variety to its limit and indeed required a diversity of over stitching, images, and fabrics as mandated in period prose and poetry. The opulence and eclectic nature of the Victorian era was reflected in these pieces often intended as a cover for a table top, a throw for the sofa or daybed rather than a traditional bedcovering (Plate 111). As Joel Sater observed in his book, *The Patchwork Quilt* (Ephrata, PA.: Science Press, 1981), Crazy quilts, as they first were practiced, were not an outgrowth of the linsey-woolsey era which produced the early whole cloth quilts but rather they were a deliberate design phenomenon that did not come from a mentality based on thrift. This design phenomenon was an outgrowth of the English arts and crafts movement of John Ruskin and William Morris (1860s) and the influence of Japanese inspired design which was popular at the Centennial Exposition (1876).

The Crazy quilt, and less so the Log Cabin types, did not initially present an attitude of simplicity and thrift but rather one of opulence and abundance, yet thrift did play a part in their making as indicated in two articles on them which appeared in contemporary farm magazines:

A crazy cushion for a chair was made of bits of gay colored worsted left from dresses. They were combined with scrap and had small figures worked on each scrap with crewel or fine Saxony yarn. The figures were first stamped. A beetle, turtle, flower or leaf was all that was on it. The scraps were then basted on a lining as large as desired, the edges turned under and then worked in pretty crazy stitches. An inner lining sewed up and filled with feathers, with cayenne pepper sprinkled among them to keep moths from them, and then inserted into the cushion that has been sewed to the underlining. This makes a very pretty cushion and uses up scraps that would probably not be used in other ways about home adornments. "Fancy Works Patterns" by Mrs. Throp/*The National Stockman and Farmer*/July 12, 1888/p.286.

One hears frequent demands for new ideas in patchwork from those who are tired of crazywork, but still wish to fashion pillows, cushions, quilts, etc. from the pretty bits of silk and velvet that will accumulate so fast. The design here given is a useful one for that purpose, for by it one can dispose of pieces of varying shapes and sizes. As represented, the small dark squares are of plain velvet, the gray ones are of watered silk, in a lighter shade, the figured ones are brilliantly-flowered brocaded satin, or velvet, and the larger parts surrounding them all, the foundation parts, are of plain gros-grain silk or satin. Cut the design into four pieces by cutting across each way diagonally from corner to corner, and one can see how each of the quarter sections may be easily pieced, then seamed together. For a pattern twelve inches square, when finished the small pieces should each be two inches square; the larger, plain portions, must be cut to match, or finish out, the pieced parts of each triangular section. This is a pretty size for a quilt; and cambrics, satins, or prints might be used if preferred. Of course, in a quilt the plain outer portions of the squares should be of two different colors or shades. Half of the squares should be finished with one color, and the other half with the other, and should then be arranged to alternate across the quilts. Inch-and-a-half squares, cut from the small sample packages one gets when buying dress goods by mail, produce a nine-inch square when completed; four of these make a pretty chair cushion. "Square for a Cushion-Cover or Quilt" by Frances H. Perry/*American Agriculturist*/February 1890/p. 79.

Women resorted to sending for packaged silk remnants when they and their friends' sewing scraps did not provide the variety required for Crazy quilts. By February 1884, as many as six companies were advertising such assortments on a single page of the *Ladies Home Journal*. Popular women's

Plate 84. Detail of Columbia County crib quilt./Pieced velvet, silk, taffeta, satin, gros grain ribbons with a moiré back. Applied solid-colored binding. 47" × 31."/ Collection of Columbia County Historical Society.

ESTATE INVENTORY OF
THOMAS DUFFEY

Three Springs, Huntingdon County
March 11, 1879

1 Hap	.75
1 Blanket	.25
1 Woolen Hap	.50
1 Quilt	1.50
1 Calico Hap	1.00
1 Blanket	1.00

ESTATE INVENTORY OF
ELIZABETH SCHOCK

West Twp. Huntingdon County
1884

1 Green & yellow quilt	$2.00
1 yellow & white quilt	$2.00
1 Green & red quilt	$2.00
1 Red & blue quilt	$2.00

ESTATE INVENTORY OF
MARGARET H. ANDERSON

Huntingdon County
Sept. 26, 1890

1 crazy quilt	25.00
1 comfort	1.50

ESTATE INVENTORY OF
CATHERINE NEARHOOF

Warriors Mark,
Huntingdon County
1900

To David Nearhoff 1 Hap, 1 Quilt,
2 sheets, 1 Bolster Case
To Mary Williams 2 sheets,
1 Bolster, 1 Quilt
To Abednego Nearhoof 2 sheets,
1 Bolster Case, 1 Quilt
To Jeremiah Nearhoof 2 sheets,
1 bolster, 1 Quilt
To Michael Nearhoof 2 sheets,
1 bolster, 1 Quilt
To James Nearhoof 2 sheets,
1 bolster, 1 Quilt
To Levi Nearhoof 2 sheets,
1 bolster case, 1 Quilt
To Ellen Bucket 2 sheets, 1 bolster
case, 1 Hap, 1 Quilt
To Metes Nearhoof 2 sheets,
1 bolster case, 1 Quilt

magazines of the period like *Godeys, Petersons,* and *Arthur's* were among the first to offer threads and pattern instructions for as many as sixty crazy stitches at one time. Dorothy Bond's book *Crazy Stitches* (Cottage Grove, Oregon: Bond, 1981) documents many of them.

But just as quickly as this design phenomenon arose starting in 1879, it was dropped by those more urban periodicals which went out to promote new types of fancy work. Other magazines, like *Good Housekeeping, The National Stockman and Farmer,* and *The American Farmer,* then took up the merits of the Crazy. Those magazines began to talk about using wools and the salvageable parts of worn clothing rather than just silks and velvets. When this became a trend—it certainly was in central Pennsylvania (Plates 112-113)—the Crazy went from being a thin silk throw in the parlor to being a warm and practical bedcovering often filled with wool batting. It remained a design type in this more restrained, ordered, and practical form as late as the 1930s. Sturdy wool examples abound unified with a single fancy stitch (feather or briar) in a single colored yarn. Gone are the sequins, beads, centennial ribbons, hat liners, and ties of the fine and fancy earlier pieces. However, like the Crazies made of silk and velvets, the wool examples are often signed and dated in contrast to all other quilt types of the same period.

While Crazy quilts' point of origin and date can be documented as Penny McMorris did in her book *Crazy Quilts* (New York: E. P. Dutton, 1984) and Virginia Gunn did in her article on nineteenth-century embroidered work in *Uncoverings 1984* (Mill Valley, CA: American Quilt Study Group, 1985), the Log Cabin's initial design source and date is elusive. It is generally felt that it emerged as a new quilt type after the Civil War. In central Pennsylvania they were executed in both exceedingly narrow or average-sized but uniform strips. They were made in silk and velvets when used for throws at the height of the Crazy period, or in wools and later cottons when constructed

full-sized as practical bedcoverings. With the exception of one pastel variation made in the 1930s (Plate 89), they were usually made of nineteenth-century fabric and did not form a continuous body of work as did the simpler country Crazy which was made through the 1930s. On the other hand, they have undergone a major and sustained revival amongst contemporary quiltmakers which the Crazy has not.

The Log Cabin quilt, unlike its counterpart in pressed-work, the Crazy quilt, was not a showpiece for embroidery stitches, hence it was not signed or dated. Its construction method interestingly evolved though from pressed-work on a foundation to a pieced tradition.

The Log Cabin variations most often seen in our area are the *Court House Steps* distantly followed by *Furrows, Windmills, Pineapples,* or *Streaks of Lightning.* Some exhibited a very wide variety of scrap fabrics within a single top while others appear to have been made largely of purchased fabric. Like the heavier wool Crazy quilts, some of the wool Log Cabins were made as thick comforts or haps—a significant departure in appearance and use from the fanciful, opulent, and less useful silk examples.

Both of these types of quilts were made by rural women who continued to make the more traditional pieced and appliqué patterns of their grandmothers and mothers. Both were made as fundraising quilts upon a rare occasion, and as doll or crib quilts. The Crazy however was seen in greater concentration in our more urban areas like Harrisburg and Williamsport, and it is still considered by many area rural families as their "best" quilt. The fancy fabric used in them even if deteriorating from tin salt disease, in addition to the abundant imagery and varied overstitching (often signed and dated), contributes to this place of high esteem. For area families, the Crazy quilt represents a distant era of urban places and taste, a contrast to the familiar frugal nature of the farm and rural crossroads community which has been a continuum in their lives.

Plate 85. *Quilt made by Kate Corman Barley Robinson b. 1842 Carlisle, Cumberland County d. 1924 Carlisle, Cumberland County. / Pieced print and solid-colored wools and cottons with solid-colored back. Applied solid-colored binding. 83" square. / Collection of G. Robert and Joyce Wrightstone.*

Fig. 25. *Kate Corman Barley Robinson.*

86

Plate 86. *Quilt made by Susanna Catherine Kerchner b. 1868 Walker Township, Juniata County d. 1947 Mifflintown, Juniata County. / Pieced solid-colored cottons with solid-colored back. Back to front as edge treatment. 66" square with 5 stitches per inch in colored thread. / Collection of Sara Walters.*

Fig. 26. *Susanna Catherine Kerchner.*

Plate 87. *Quilt made by Jenny Rhine
b. Delaware Township, Juniata
County d. McAlisterville, Juniata
County. / Pieced solid-colored silks
with solid-colored back. Applied silk
binding.* 64" *square. / Collection of
Barbara Tennis Schlegel.*

*While working as a seamstress at
Strawbridge's in Philadelphia, Jenny
Rhine saved scraps of material used
in the lining of men's jackets and
made them into this Log Cabin quilt
in* 1892. *In* 1906 *she gave it to her
mother's great aunt in whose family
it has been passed on.*

88

Plate 88. *Detail of quilt made by Clara Hagenbuch b. ca.1855 Center Township, Columbia County d. ca.1938 Berwick, Columbia County. / Pieced print and calico cottons with print back. Back brought to front as edge treatment. 85" × 72" with 4-6 stitches per inch. / Collection of Hortense E. Hagenbuch.*

Fig. 27. *Ida, Sarah, and Clara Hagenbuch.*

89

Plate 89. *Detail of quilt made by Susie Reed Martin b. 1894 and d. 1972 in Cumberland County. / Pieced solid-colored cottons with white back. Back brought to front as edge treatment. 72" square with 8 stitches per inch. / Collection of Florence Smith.*

Fig. 28. *Susie Reed Martin (standing), her husband, and Florence Smith.*

90

Plate 90. *Quilt made by Mary Fraker Meyers b. 1875 Cloversburg, Cumberland County d. 1964 Carlisle, Cumberland County. Pieced print and calico cottons with apron gingham back. Back brought to front as edge treatment. 86" × 72" with 7-9 stitches per inch. / Collection of Ella Killinger Pechart.*

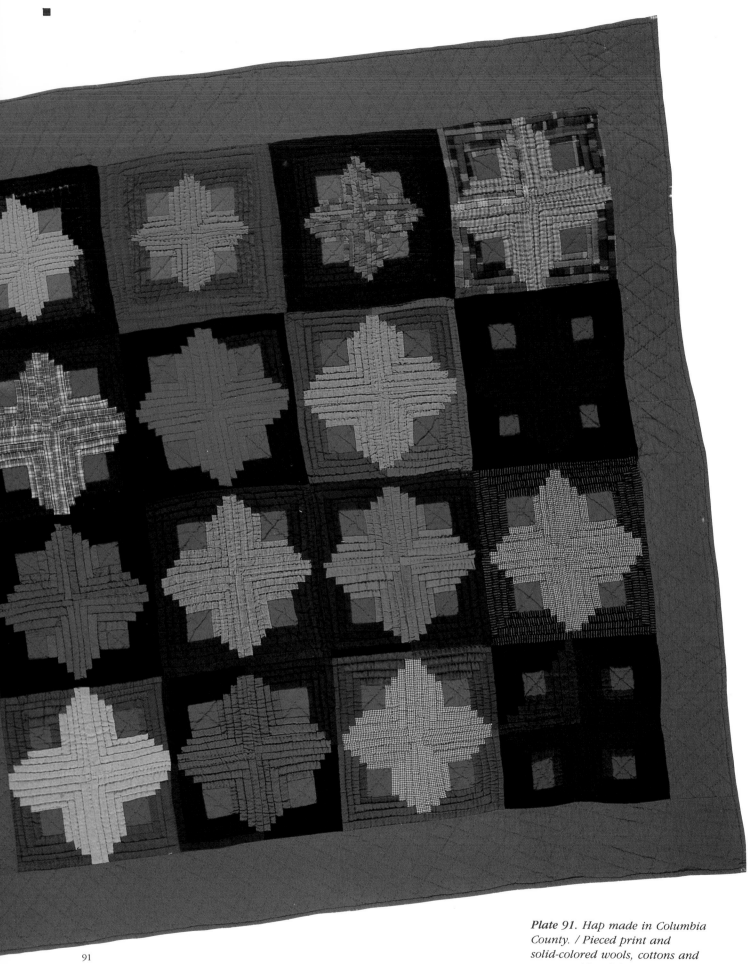

Plate 91. Hap made in Columbia County. / Pieced print and solid-colored wools, cottons and rayons with solid-colored back. 74¹/₂" × 72¹/₂" with 4-5 stitches per inch in colored thread. / Collection of Betty Apple.

Plate 92. *Pillow cover made by Sarah Ann Proctor Eckels b. 1820 Carlisle, Cumberland County d. 1899 Carlisle, Cumberland County. / Pieced solid-colored silks with silk back. Applied solid-colored silk binding. 17" × 17½." / Collection of Barbara Marbain.*

Plate 93. *Crib quilt made by Caroline B. Bistline b. 1841 Perry County d. 1922 Cumberland County. / Pieced solid-colored wools with print back. 49" × 37" and tied. / Collection of Caroline Bistline Orner.*

Fig. 29. *Caroline and George Bistline.*

92

93

Plates 94-97. *Cumberland County quilt. / Pieced and applied print and solid-colored cottons with print back. Front brought to back as edge treatment. 82" × 76½" with 5 stitches per inch. Crewel work and French knots in colored threads. / Collection of Virginia Dougherty Goodyear.*

Central Medallion quilts were popular in Cumberland County both in the early blue and white Sawtooth *variations and in early* Bethlehem Stars *(Plates 8 and 11). Later, in the Victorian era, the Central Medallion was translated into the Crazy quilt (Plates 98-99) as well as this unusual Log Cabin. Within this Central Medallion is an elaborate bouquet and a border chain in crewel work. Applied fabric pieces surround the bouquet and some are of cheater cloth; many are carefully cut out according to their printed/patterned surface.*

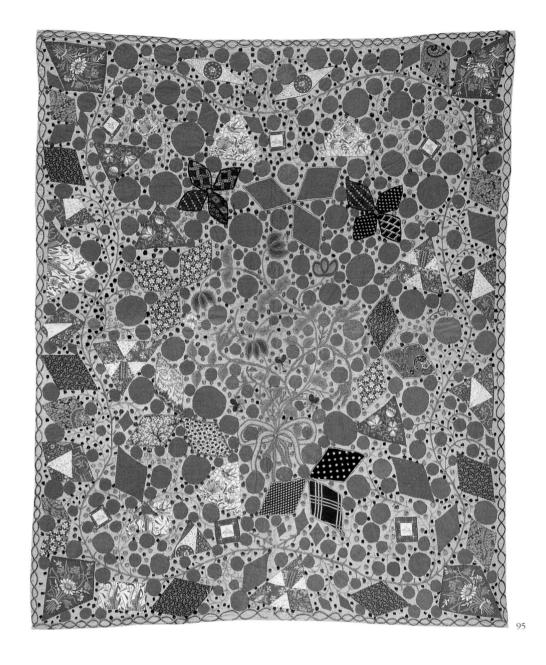

95

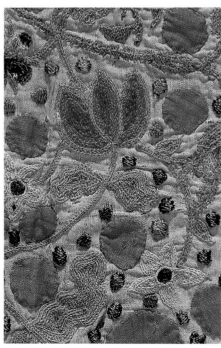

96

97

SCANDAL
"WHAT do you think....." "I'm sure I don't know."
"Don't tell anybody!!" "Oh no!! Oh no!!"

Plates 98 and 99. Cumberland County quilt. / Pieced and applied silks, and velvets with solid-colored back. Back and front turned in as edge treatment. 59½″ × 75½″ with fancy stitches in colored threads and tinsel. / Collection of Lucille Melton.

The large center square, with its two young girls in mop caps and their conversation embroidered under the word "Scandal," is surrounded by forty-eight other squares. The girls talk, "What do you think?" "I'm sure I don't know," the one replies. "Don't tell anybody!" "Oh no" "Oh no." Around the gossips are pieced and applied velvets, silks and satins with fancy stitching, some of which follows the elaborately woven fabric patterns. Twelve Kate Greenway figures are outline embroidered in different colored threads. Many of them are children playing with hoops. The unusual deep scalloped border is trimmed in multicolored thread and further embroidery.

100

Plate 100. Cumberland County quilt signed and dated "1897/VIOLET ALMEDA BRENIZE" in counted cross stitch. / Pieced print and solid-colored wool, crepes, and silks. Solid-colored back with binding. 68" × 72" with 7-9 stitches per inch and cross stitch in colored threads. / Collection of Candy Pechart Sailhamer.

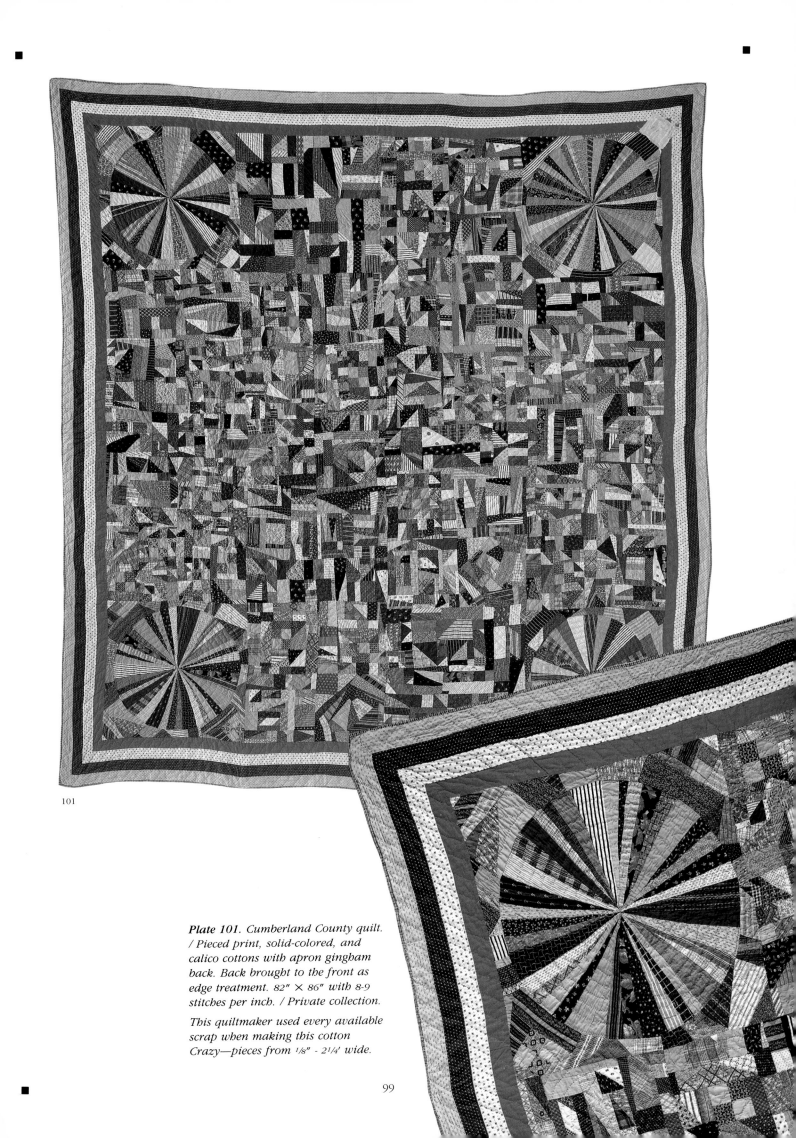

101

Plate 101. *Cumberland County quilt.
/ Pieced print, solid-colored, and
calico cottons with apron gingham
back. Back brought to the front as
edge treatment. 82" × 86" with 8-9
stitches per inch. / Private collection.*

*This quiltmaker used every available
scrap when making this cotton
Crazy—pieces from 1/8" - 21/4' wide.*

Plate 102. *Detail from quilt made by Mary Melissa Diehl Miller b. 1840 Mahoning Township, Montour County d. 1910 Turbotville, Northumberland County. / Pieced silks and velvets with print back. Back brought to front as edge treatment. 70" × 60", dated "1887" and signed "MDM" in elaborate embroidery stitches. / Collection of Howard and Andrew Sechler.*

102

103

Plate 103. *Detail of Huntingdon County quilt. / Pieced silks and velvets with solid-colored back. Front brought to back as edge treatment. 63" square. / Painted and embroidered images; two blocks with figures formed in part with paper scraps. / Collection of Huntingdon County Historical Society.*

Plate 104: (upper right) Another detail from Plate 103.

Plate 105. (lower right) Detail of quilt top made by Anna Sechler Landis and her friends from Mt. Union, Huntingdon County and dated "April 15, 1895 / Mt. Union / Pa." Also shown in Plate 59. Pieced silks and velvets with fancy stitches in colored threads with beads, sequins, and painted images. 62" square. / Collection of LaRue L. Obler.

Plates 106 and 107. (far right) Details of quilt top made by Clara Jane Robb Ward b. 1846 McConnelstown, Huntingdon County d. 1923 McConnelstown, Huntingdon County. / Pieced silks and velvets with fancy stitches in colored threads. 58" × 60." / Collection of Donna Leamer.

Plate 108. Table piece made by Nancy Wetzler Bashore b. 1838 McAlisterville, Juniata County d. 1922 McAlisterville, Juniata County. / Pieced velvets with fancy stitches in colored threads. 11" square with lace trim. / Collection of Jane Bashore Marhefka.

104

106

105

107

108

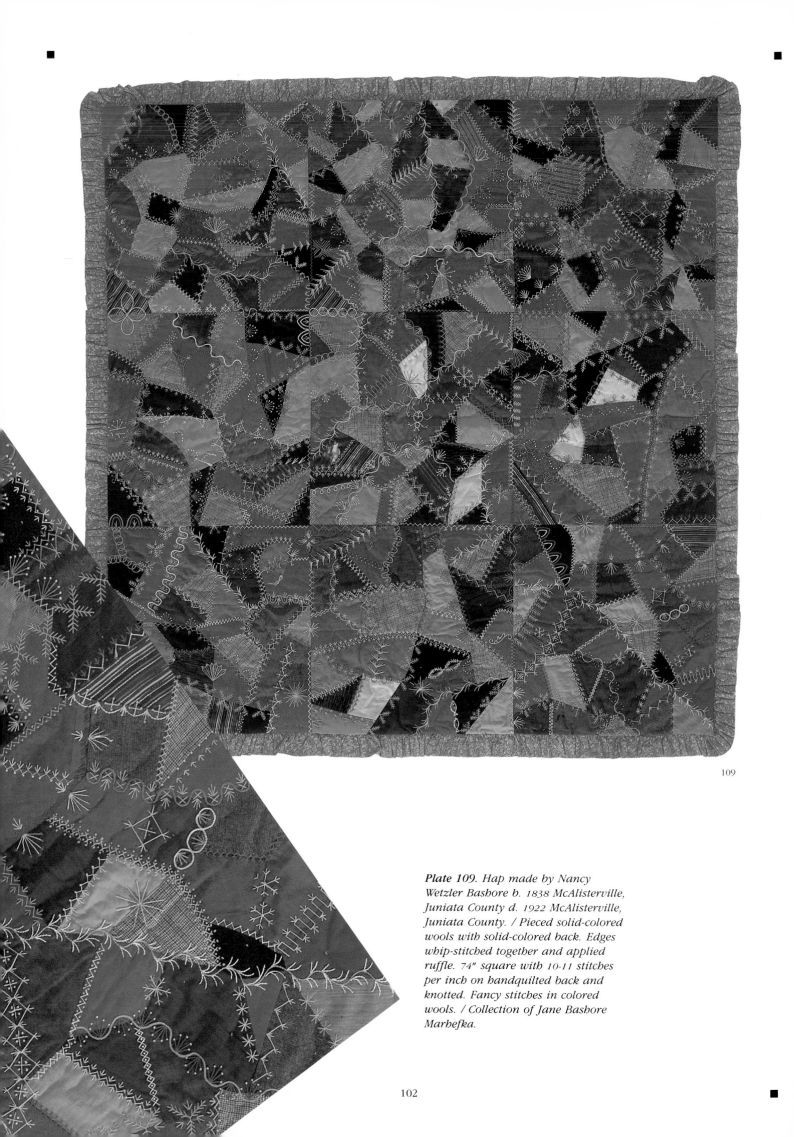

Plate 109. *Hap made by Nancy
Wetzler Bashore b. 1838 McAlisterville,
Juniata County d. 1922 McAlisterville,
Juniata County. / Pieced solid-colored
wools with solid-colored back. Edges
whip-stitched together and applied
ruffle. 74" square with 10-11 stitches
per inch on handquilted back and
knotted. Fancy stitches in colored
wools. / Collection of Jane Bashore
Marhefka.*

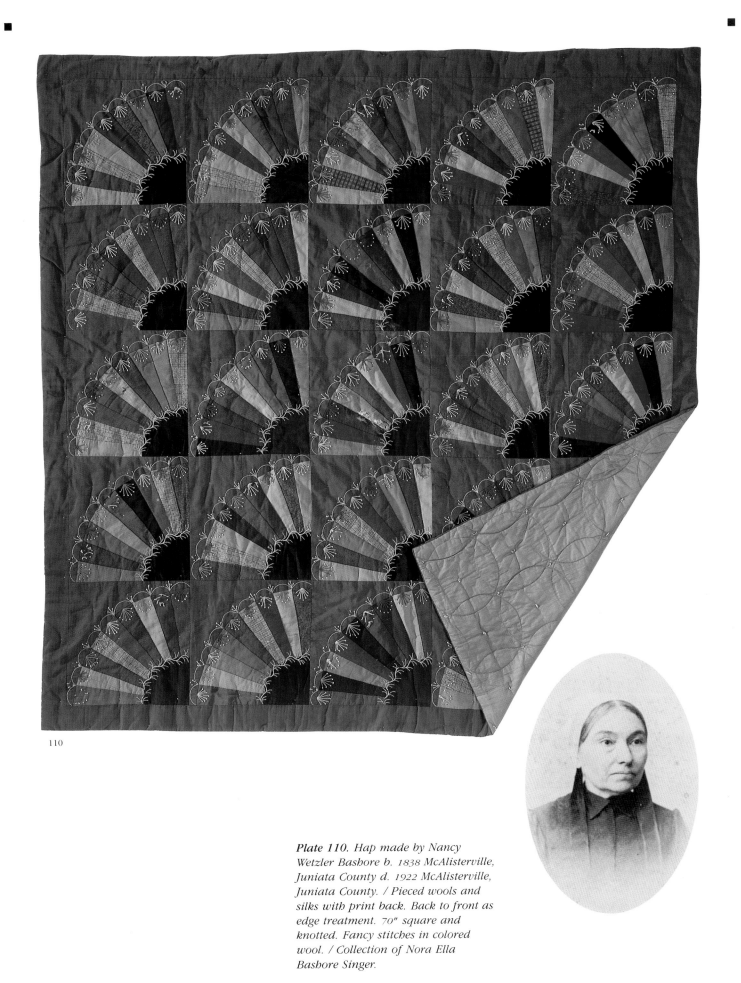

110

Plate 110. *Hap made by Nancy Wetzler Bashore b.* 1838 *McAlisterville, Juniata County d.* 1922 *McAlisterville, Juniata County. / Pieced wools and silks with print back. Back to front as edge treatment.* 70" *square and knotted. Fancy stitches in colored wool. / Collection of Nora Ella Bashore Singer.*

Fig. 30. *Nancy Wetzler Bashore.*

THE COLONIAL REVIVAL

In the October 1894 issue of *The Ladies Home Journal*, author Sybil Lanigen wrote a lengthy article on pieced quilt designs called "Revival of the Patchwork Quilt." As she noted, "The vagaries of fashion are unaccountable and no one can tell in what direction they will lead next. Of late months everything which could be recognized as old-fashioned is the new fashion . . . The decree has gone forth that a revival of patchwork quilts is at hand, and dainty fingers whose owners have known only patches and patchworks from family description are busy placing the blocks together in new and artistic patterns, as well as in the real old-time order." Indeed, since the late 1880s, there had been occasional mention of "grandmother's" type patchwork, as contrasted to the silk and velvet Crazy quilt phenomenon, but it was Lanigen who first coined the return to "mosaics of calico" as a revival. The patterns she presented in 1894 were a *Nine Patch* variation, the *Bethlehem Star*, a *Central Medallion* pattern, and *Flying Geese*, all in contrast to ". . . the rock of ugliness and the whirlpool of intricacy," or the Crazy quilt.

Only two years later, periodicals like the *National Stockman and Farmer*, *The Hearthstone*, *The Hearth and Home*, and *The American Agriculturalist* joined *The Ladies Home Journal* in praising the use of woolen and cotton scraps, in advocating the purchase of good, dye-fast materials in quiltmaking, in telling of old-fashioned quilting bees, as well as in publishing dozens of quilting patterns and patches. The Ladies Art Company in St. Louis, Missouri starting in 1889 was sending out hundreds of different pieced and appliquéd pattern designs and sample blocks.

Author Alice Morse Earl, who researched and promoted colonial life, including quiltmaking, nonetheless found the amount of labor in the cutting, fitting and quilting "almost painful to regard," *Home Life in Colonial Days* (New York: Macmillan Company, 1898). But within only a few years, others like Helen Blair in an article, "Dower Chest Treasures," in *House Beautiful* (February 1904) felt that "If, however one has not preserved the work of some piecing and quilting ancestress, she may, 'an' it please her,' fall herself apiecing." As she noted, "The old quilts which are reappearing under such interesting circumstances are, many of them, quite worthy of their recall to consequence. The colors are often old hand-dyes, the patterns marvels of design, and the quilting intricately beautiful. One of these old quilts, into which a woman of long ago put so much creative and adaptive skill, will give an air to even the most commonplace of modern beds. It will glorify a beautiful old bed." And on such an affirmative note, the revival of quiltmaking as done by one's grandmother was well on its way. A revival, not of something that had died out completely (for that was not the case) but rather, a revival of an earlier tradition within quiltmaking. It was the revival of the less urban wool or cotton pieced and appliquéd quilt patterns, patterns which had been usurped by the urban silk and velvet Crazy and pressed-work quilts of the 1870s and 1880s.

This age of discovery and rediscovery of quiltmaking traditions coincided with a period in American architecture and furnishings called the "colonial revival." It was a period, as Kenneth Ames notes in the introduction to Winterthur's *The Colonial Revival in America* (New York: W. W. Norton & Company, 1985), either narrowly defined as existing between the nation's Centennial and "the advent of the modern movement of the early twentieth century," or "encompassing virtually any variety of artifactual interaction with visions of colonial America." Quiltmaking was involved in the colonial revival in both the narrow and the broad sense as defined by Ames and other authors in the accompanying essays. In this limited space we will deal with the former.

One of the first harbingers of the colonial revival was in the colonial kitchens that were presented to the public at the large Sanitary Fairs used to raise funds for the Union Army (see Rodris Roth's article "The New England, or 'Olde Tyme,' Kitchen Exhibit at Nineteenth-Century Fairs," in *The Colonial Revival in America*). They often had quiltings in them along with articles and food that were attempts to transport one back to simpler, stabler and more patriotic times. As noted in *The New York Times* of June 19, 1864, in describing such a kitchen at the Sanitary Commission's Fair in Philadelphia:

The Pennsylvania Kitchen is a snug little affair. Here you can make yourself perfectly at home, and eat, with a decided relish, the different articles which are displayed before you. The "Bill of Fare" consists of latwerg, noodle soup, etwas, funner-wurst-waffles, trichter-kutchen (funnel cakes), and numerous other delicacies which delight the palates of a real old-fashioned Pennsylvania Dutchman. This kitchen is a great feature of the fair, and a visit to it provokes that hearty good feeling and enjoyableness which more elegant apartments sometimes fail to excite.

Indeed, this interest in the founding fathers and their times and lifestyles became a full-fledged revival twenty years later. It was handled differently in various ladies' periodicals according to their audience. In magazines like *Hearth and Home*, *The Rural New Yorker*, *Farm and Fireside*, and *The Progressive Farmer*, the reintroduction of old pieced quilt patterns (i.e. colonial) is presented as a swapping of news

Fig. 32. Esther Derr Sandel

Plate 111. *Detail of quilt made by Esther Derr Sandel b.1915 Hemlock Township, Columbia County./Pieced and applied solid-colored cottons on white top with solid-colored back. Applied solid-colored binding. 72" × 88" with 8 stitches per inch./Collection of maker. This* Johnny Jump-up, *a Ruby Short McKim pattern, was made in 1935 when Esther Derr Sandel was nineteen and just married.*

amongst friends (or readers). On the other hand, in those magazines which were reaching a mixed and often more urban audience, the same quilt was presented as "old-fashioned" and quaint. By 1910 Clara Stone, who derived many quilt patterns from *Hearth and Home*, published 186 of them in her "Practical Needlework-Quilt Patterns," many of them different from those already available from the Ladies Art Company.

Clara Stone's catalog as well as "Martha Washington's Patchwork Book" (1916), "Aunt Jane's Prize-Winning Quilt Designs" in *The Household Journal* (1916), "Colonial Patchwork" by Artamo Thread (1916) and Joseph Doyle Company's The Patchwork Companion" (1911), all quickly appeared to help the new quiltmaker discover a legitimately old-time quilt to her liking or to aid an older quiltmaker in rediscovering one. "Grandmother," "Mother," "Romance," "Patriotism," and "Colonial" were interwoven into one package, sometimes literally wrapped together as on quilt batting wrappers by Mountain Mist and later the Lockport Batting Company. Following on the heels of Martha Washington and Aunt Jane, were companies called Aunt Martha, Virginia Snow, and Grandmother Clark's, all commercial ventures established to meet the insatiable needs of quiltmakers after World War I.

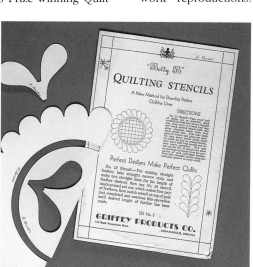

Magazines such as *Good Housekeeping* and *The Designer* in particular promoted the look of the colonial quilt, sometimes at the expense of practicality. For instance in May 1923, *The Designer* showed how, by constructing barrel hoops expanded to the width of one's bed and covered with chicken wire, one could build a support for a patchwork quilt that would imitate an old-fashioned feather bed. On a more practical note, the Louisville Bedding Company advertising in *Good Housekeeping* (April 1928) claimed that:

Plates 112 and 113. Quilting stencils and Dresden Plate quilt pattern. / Stailey collection.

Day by day, the magic and beauty of Colonial America is making its way into the modern house. Olde Kentucky Quilts are a delightful result of this desire to recapture the charm of Early American house furnishings. No quest for antiques is more eagerly pursued today than the quest for quilts—the uniquely patterned and brightly colored bed coverings that were the pride of our grandmothers. Unfortunately, few of the old quilts remain. Fortunately, the finest of the old treasures have become models for Olde Kentucky Quilts. So that now, at a very moderate cost, every bedroom in your house may be fitted with its own particular pattern and color. Olde Kentucky Quilts are rich in tradition and are true to their noble ancestry. Each design is faithfully copied from an antique quilt.

A year later, the company invoked the name of Priscilla Alden, one of our staid Pilgrim ancestors, and created an image of her too busy for primping as she would have been cooking, sewing, spinning, weaving and quilting for John and their eleven children.

Florid poetry and prose about quilts was not limited to such advertisements. Some, like Sarah Wilson Middleton's ode to "Grandmother's Quilt," (p. 107) were being rediscovered in *The Romance of the Patchwork Quilt in America* (Caldwell, Idaho: Caxton Printers Ltd., 1935). Such examples are numerous and they continued from the 1880s through the 1930s. It is no wonder that in the middle of this (1924) Carlie Sexton, one of the revival's first promoters, cried out "enough" when she called much of her contemporaries' quilt work "reproductions."

The 1880s through the 1930s was a time when the media, usually farm and women's magazines, could promote this revival through prose, poetry, and instructions in addition to commercial advertisements. Such magazines (and newspapers in the Mid-west) also promoted for the first time the designs and work of specific women and as a result Anne Orr, Ruby Short McKim, Eveline Foland, Rose Kretsinger, and Charlotte Whitehill, among others, became household names, synonymous with different aspects in the quilt's revival. Some of these women viewed quilts as one way of being artistic, of making objects of superior design; some did quilts exclusively.

Designer Anne Orr's patterns began to be seen in *The Southern Woman* in the early days of World War I while she was its art editor. In 1919 she became the Art-Needlework editor for *Good Housekeeping* and each month a page of her recommendations and designs (at first traditional patterns and then her own starting in 1929) were featured until she retired in 1940. She operated "The Anne Orr Studio" in Nashville, Tennessee, which published over seventy needlework books and pamphlets including many quilt patterns which she always had her group of women try first. One could order the instructions for her new designs, both geometric and hard-edged as well as realistic, or one could order stamped or basted tops, hot iron transfers, or—if one hadn't the time— a completed quilt done by craftswomen in Kentucky.

The Jonquil was one of Anne Orr's most loved designs (Plate 118) and the one seen in the greatest number in central Pennsylvania. Her appliqués always had a dominant central focus and a border which was rarely straight-edged. She also introduced a revolutionary new concept: that one's blocks need not be of uniform size. Many of her earlier patterns were based on shaded fabric squares which when assembled, looked like large scale counted cross-stitch as her *Dresden Star Flower* (1936), *Oval Wreath* (1935), *Star Flower*, and *Marie Antoinette* (1936).

Anne Orr's statement in 1925 that "the most important piece of furniture in a bedroom is, of course, the bed. There, the most important accessory is the bedspread. Upon it the eyes are fixed on entering a bedroom, and upon it one's interest centers," was echoed by others like Ruby Short McKim who designed many quilts. Her *Johnny Jump-Up* (Plate 111) was one of many pieced flowers she designed, all very hard-edged and very individual in concept *(Oriental Poppy, Pieced Rose, Pieced Pansy, Pieced Iris,* and *Beautiful Tulip).* Ruby Short McKim was trained as a designer, graduating from Parson Art School in New York in 1910. She returned to her home state of Missouri where she and her husband set up the McKim Studios which made and sold newspaper features on, among other things, comics and quiltmaking. The studio became a mail-order outlet for their needlework items.

Like Anne Orr, Ruby McKim became an Art Needlework editor, in this case, for *Better Homes and Gardens.* She also paralleled her contemporary in that she was not a needleworker herself but had her ideas executed by others. Like Orr, she started designing straight pieced quilt projects, particularly concentrating on the problem of transposing flowers into that mode, however, she also evolved interesting but simple curved-work appliqué patterns. As with Orr, her blocks were not always uniform, and when square were usually set on their point. Ruby McKim may have been the first to realize that the new quiltmakers (of the 1930s) might not have the room nor the inclination to work on a large quilt frame and she was an advocate for what she called "apartment quilting," now called "lap quilting."

Following in Ruby Short McKim's footsteps as the quilt pattern illustrator for *The Kansas City Star* was another important quilt designer, Eveline Smith Foland. Starting in 1929 her initials appear on some of the newspaper's quilt patterns and late in 1932 they appear to be done exclusively by Foland. One of her first series of quilt designs was *Santa's Parade in a Nursery,* followed by *Memory Bouquet* and *The Horn of Plenty.* Like some of the earlier McKim patterns these quilts employed different appliquéd or embroidered images unified by a central theme. Although her designs and those of Edna Marie Dunn, who continued the quilt pattern section, appeared in this mid-western newspaper exclusively, their patterns were traded and sent to friends or relatives back East and to other parts of the country. One of the more popular of Eveline Foland's patterns was *Ararat,* a pieced elephant design (1931) done after an elephant at Kansas City's Swope Park Zoo. Another favorite pieced animal pattern was *Giddap,* a donkey designed with the 1932 presidential campaign in mind.

Realistic rather than abstract images became popular in this time period. New pieced and appliquéd patterns such as *Johnny Jump-Up* (Plate 111) and the *Colonial Dame* (Plate 120) in addition to the appliquéd theme quilts such as Eveline Foland's *Santa's Parade* are examples. In these quilts little is left to the imagination: buttons are embroidered on appliquéd dresses, actual cloth hankies hang out of *Overall Sam's* pockets, or the quiltmaker carefully cuts her fabric to show her *Sunbonnet Sue's* watering can (Plate 119) (read Betty Hagerman's *Sunbonnet Sues* on the proliferation and evolution of this popular new pattern).

Ode to Grandmother's Quilt

"Some day,
We will have a square for you."
She would say; and to me, standing by her knee
In that old-fashioned sitting room
With its forgotten horsehair,
Flowered carpeting,
And firelit hearth
Of childhood memory,
She would explain
That homemade tapestry:

"That pretty printed one
Was once your mother's dress;
The pink, Aunt Julia's,
And the blue, a shirt of Uncle Will's;
While all the corners were begun
With Kansas scraps Aunt Hannah sent
From where the Indians live,
Beneath the prairie sun;
And that old piece of fancy cloth
Was Uncle Albert's vest,
And all those fill-ins at the seams
Were ties of Grandpa's,
Long, long years ago . . . ."

But mine—I thought with childlike dreams—
Should be a very large square,
And of pink brocade;
When I had become great and made
The whole wide world
To tremble at my name!
When I would have fame,
And be as high as the topmost steeple
Of the village spires,
When from all lands would come the people
Just to hear me sing.
Then would Grandmother bring
From out it's lavender that quilt of yore,
And pointing to that pink brocade
Square of gorgeousness,
Say, with prideful happiness,
"This . . . . my famous grandchild wore!"

But now—
If only she may find
Upon my quilt of life,
A little, humble patch of white—
Of righteousness.

Sarah Wilson, Middleton

The earliest quilt type to have had such representational images and/or themes were those made of Turkey red thread outline-embroidered images on white whole cloth (Plate 121). Doris Albright started embroidering her patches as an eleven-year-old and completed the figures—which represented the days of the week and the months of the year—one year later, in 1932. That would have been in the last stages of using red outlined images—a trend which had begun in the 1880s as a decorative approach to dresser scarves and pillow shams.

Favorite traditional patterns, the *Rose of Sharon* and the *Bethlehem Star,* were rediscovered and modified in the 1920s and 1930s. Others such as the *Basket,* executed as both a realistic and an abstract pattern (Plates 114-115), appeared in substantial numbers starting in the 1880s—as did the *Schoolhouse* and *House* patterns. (The earliest documented *Basket* we found was one made in Alvina, Snyder County, in 1856. All others dated from the 1880s on, or the colonial revival period. In the recent Tennessee quilt project, one was found made in the 1840's and another ca. 1863.)

Also in the twentieth century one sees for the first time the emergence of regionally or nationally-known quiltmaker/artists. Charlotte Jane Whitehill, Rose G. Kretsinger, Hannah Haynes Headlee, and Bertha Stenge (see *Quilters' Newsletter Magazine* 1971 pp. 4-6, December 1977 pp. 24-25,29; January 1980 cover; February 1980 pp. 12-13,18). They might all be called, as Bertha Stenge has been, "the Michelangelo[s] of the quilt world, (QNM, 1971)."

Another development was the moving of exhibits of quilts from the county fair to the university and decorative arts museums with the University of Kansas (1920) and the Newark Museum (1914) leading the way. These shows were curated by pioneers Sallie Casey Thayer and John Cotton Dana, respectively. And last but not least, the quilt became a subject for serious study. As Cuesta Benbury notes in her article "The 20th Century's First Quilt Revival Part II," (*Quilters Newsletter Magazine,* September 1979 pp. 25-26,29), Fanny Bergen, Charlotte Boldtman, Frances Garside, Mrs. Leopold Simon, and Elizabeth Daingerfield all wrote informative historical quilt articles from 1908-1911. They were forerunners by only a few years of Marie Webster and her important book *Quilts: Their Story and How to Make Them,* (New York: Doubleday, Page and Company, 1915), the first book on quilts published in America, and an important work still. It was followed by others, most notably *Old Patchwork Quilts and The Women Who Made Them* (1929) by Ruth Findley, *The Romance of the Patchwork Quilt in America* (1935) by Carrie A. Hall and Rose G. Kretsinger, and by the influential articles of Florence Peto.

In large part, this first revival in quiltmaking could not have existed without a media receptive to being a forum for the discussion of quilt patterns of "grandmother's time." Patterns such as those of Mrs. John Ebersole (cover) were traded, shared, tried and loved again.

114

Plate 114. *Quilt made by Susan Anne Bashore Stouffer b. 1850 Wertsville, Cumberland County d. 1936 Lower Cumberland, Cumberland County. / Pieced print, solid-colored, and calico cottons with print back. Back* brought to front as an edge treatment. *71″ × 68″ with 8-9 stitches per inch. / Private collection.*

Fig. 32. *Susan Bashore Stouffer.*

Plate 115. *Cumberland County
crib quilt. / Pieced and applied
solid-colored silks and satins with
solid-colored back. Back and front
turned in as edge treatment. 50″ ×
38″ with embroidery in colored
threads. / Collection of Betty S. Kosco.*

116

Plate 116. *Quilt commissioned by Pearl Imler of Huntingdon, Huntingdon County in the 1920s. / Pieced and applied solid-colored chintz cottons with white back.*

Applied solid-colored binding. 84" × 107" with 10-12 stitches per inch and blanket stitching in black thread. / Collection of Barbara Harrington.

Plate 117. Quilt made by Minnie
Mowery Hudleson b. *1878* Mifflin
Township, Columbia County d. *1966*
Berwick, Columbia County. / Pieced
solid-colored cottons on white top
with white back. Back brought to

front as edge treatment. *74″ × 76″*
with *6-7* stitches per inch. / Collection
of Jane W. Soberick.

Fig. 33. Minnie Mowery Hudleson
(on right).

118

Plate 118. Quilt made by Anna
Sechler Landis b. *1876* Mount Union,
Huntingdon County d. *1947* Mount
Union, Huntingdon County. / Applied
solid-colored cottons on solid-colored
top with solid-colored back. Applied
solid-colored binding. *92″ × 82″* with
7 stitches per inch, initialed and dated
"LSLO *1935*" in colored cross stitch. /
Collection of LaRue L. Ohler.

Anna Landis made this typical *1930s*
appliqué for her grandaughter
LaRue's wedding. Like many women
of that era, Anna Landis did most of
the family's sewing and mending in
addition to the alterations and
tailoring of others.

Plate 119. Detail of quilt made by Ella May Magargel Sheets b. 1865 Lairdsville, Lycoming County d. 1933 Hills Grove, Sullivan County. / Pieced print, solid-colored, and calico cottons with white back. Back brought to front as edge treatment. 71" × 81" with 7 stitches per inch. / Collection of Carol Magargel St. Clair.

Plate 120. Detail of quilt made by Minnie Mowery Hudleson b. 1878 Mifflin Township, Columbia County d. 1966 Berwick, Columbia County. / Applied print and solid-colored cottons on white top with solid-colored back. Back brought to front as an edge treatment. 76½" square with 7 stitches per inch. / Collection of Jayne W. Soberick.

119

120

Plate 121. Detail of quilt made by Doris Maxine Albright McClintock b. 1920 Mechanicsburg, Cumberland County. / Pieced solid-colored and white cottons with white back. Back brought to front as edge treatment. 90" × 84" with 9 stitches per inch. / Collection of the maker.

Most quilts have a story. As this quiltmaker noted: "I embroidered the patches for this quilt the summers of 1931 and 1932, when I was eleven and twelve years old. My parents had a poultry farm and hatchery (Albright's Poultry Farm and Hatchery) just south of Mechanicsburg, Cumberland County, Pennsylvania. The village was known as Kohlertown. I was a pupil at the Kohlertown School, now the Little Theatre of Mechanicsburg.

During the summer months, April through August, I walked in to Mechanicsburg to take piano lessons. After my piano lesson I would stop at Brincle's, a little gift and notion shop on Main Street, and select the patches for this quilt.

When my son was about the age I was when I embroidered the patches in this quilt, he wanted it on his bed. At first I was reluctant to put it on his bed, but he was always a careful child and I thought to myself, 'What am I saving it for?' I'm so glad I did put it on his bed for several months, because he died August 4, 1985, and so my question was answered."

Fig. 34. Doris Maxine Albright McClintock

121

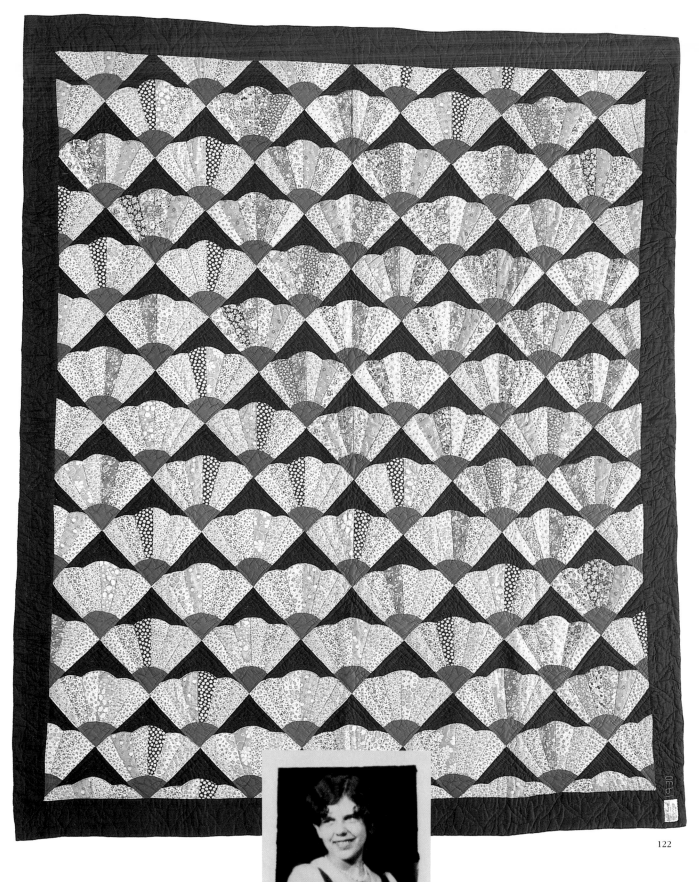

Plate 122. *Quilt made by Mary C.
Stabnau b. 1911 Port Royal,
Cumberland County. / Pieced print
and solid-colored cottons with
solid-colored back. Slip stitched as
edge treatment. 80″ × 68″ with 6
stitches per inch in colored thread. /
Collection of the maker.*

*In 1931 friends gave Mary Stabnau
small patches to make a "Friendship
Fan" reproduced elsewhere as an* Art
Deco Fan—*a newly introduced period
pattern.*

Fig. 35. *Mary C. Stabnau*

Plate 123. *Quilt made by Mary Ellen Klinger Saylor b. 1845 Perry County. d. 1925 Perry County. / Pieced solid-colored and white cottons with white back. Back brought to front as an edge treatment. 72" × 90" with 8 stitches per inch. / Collection of Patricia Hench.*

This flag quilt was made for and with the help of William Saylor Hench (b. 1894) by his grandmother when he was ten years old.

123

BIBLIOGRAPHY

Albacete, M.J., and Sharon D'Atri and Jane Reeves. *Ohio Quilts/A Living Tradition*. Canton, Ohio: The Canton Art Institute, 1981.

Alberta Quilts. Edmonton, Canada: Provincial Museum of Alberta, 1984.

Album of Favorite Quilting Designs. Pittsburgh: Pennsylvania Farmer, n.d.

The American Agriculturalist, 1800-1905.

The American Cultivator. 1839-1850.

American Farmer. 1819-1897.

"Ann Orr-She Captured Beauty." *"Quilters Newsletter Magazine*. June 1973, pp. 12-16, 27.

Arthur's Home Magazine or *The American Home Magazine,* 1852-1898.

Avery, Virginia. "Florence Peto-Renaissance Woman of Mid-Century." *Quilters Newsletter Magazine*. January 1980, pp. 16-18, 26.

Bacon, Lenice Ingram. *American Patchwork Quilts*. New York: William Morrow & Co., Inc., 1973.

Bank, Mirra. *Anonymous Was a Woman*. New York: St. Martins Press, 1979.

Benberry, Cuesta. "Charm Quilts." *Quilters Newsletter Magazine*. March 1980, pp. 14-15.

——————— , "The 20th Century's First Quilt Revival," *Quilters Newsletter Magazine*. July/August 1979, pp. 20-22; September 1979, pp. 25, 26, 29; October 1979, pp. 10-11.

"Bertha Stenge, 'The Quilting Queen of Chicago.' " *Quilters Newsletter Magazine,* 1971, pp. 4-6.

Betterton, Sheila. *The American Quilt Tradition*. The American Museum in Britain, 1976.

Binney, Edward, III and Gail Binney-Winslow. *Homage to Amanda/Two Hundred Years of American Quilts*. San Francisco: RK Press, 1984.

Bishop, Robert and Patricia Colbentz. *News Discoveries in American Quilts*. New York: Dutton, 1975.

Bond, Dorothy. *Crazy Quilt Stitches*. Cottage Grove, Oregon: Bond, 1981.

Bowen, Helen. "The Ancient Art of Quilting" *Antiques*. March 1923, pp. 113-117.

——————— . "Corded and Padded Quilting" *Antiques,* November 1924, pp. 250-253.

Brackman, Barbara. "Charlotte Jane Whitehill-Applique Artist." *Quilters Newsletter Magazine,* April 1980, pp. 23-25.

——————— . "Dating Old Quilts Parts I-III." *The Quilters Newsletter Magazine*. September 1984, pp. 24-25, 45: October 1984, pp. 26-27; November/December 1984, pp. 16-17.

Bresenhan, Karoline Patterson and Nancy Bryant Puentes. *Lone Stars/A Legacy of Texas Quilts 1836-1936*. Austin, Texas: University of Texas Press, 1986.

Burnham, Dorothy K. *Pieced Quilts of Ontario*. Toronto: Royal Ontario Museum, 1975.

Carlisle, Lillian Baker. *Pieced Work and Applique Quilts at Shelburne Museum*. Shelburne, Vermont: Shelburne Museum, 1957.

Catalog of Patchwork Quilts. Chicago, Illinois: Needlecraft Supply Co., 1939.

Caulfield, S.F.A. and Blanche C. Saward, *The Dicionary of Needlework, An Encyclopedia of Artistic, Plain and Fancy Needlework*. London: L. Upcott Gill, 1882.

Child, Lydia Maria. *The Girls Own Book*. New York: Clark Austin, 1833.

Clabburn, Pamela. *Patchwork*. Aylesbury, England: Shire Publications, 1983.

Clark, Mary Washington. *Kentucky Quilts and Their Makers*. Lexington: University Press of Kentucky, 1976.

Clark, Rickey. *Quilts and Carousels: Folk Art in the Firelands*. Oberlin, Ohio: Firelands Association for the Visual Arts, 1983.

Colby, Averil. *Patchwork*. London: B.T. Batsford. Ltd., 1958.

——————— . *Quilting*. New York: Charles Scribner's Sons, 1971.

Columbia Democrat. April 6, 1861-August 6, 1864.

Cooper, Patricia and Norma Bradley Buferd. *The Quilters. Women And Domestic Art*. Garden City, New York: Doubleday & Company, Inc., 1977.

Cozart, Dorothy. *Quilts, Cars and Trains*. Enid, Oklahoma: The Heritage League, 1985.

Curtis, Phillip. *American Quilts*. Newark, New Jersey: Newark Museum, 1973.

Dauphin County Folk Festival Program. 1939, 1949.

Davidson, Mildred. *American Quilts From the Art Institute of Chicago*. Chicago: The Art Institute of Chicago, 1966.

The Delineator or *The Designer and The Women's Magazine*. 1895-1926.

Demorest's Family Magazine. 1886-1888.

Duncan, Ruby Hinson. "A Meeting of the Sunbonnet Children I and II." *Quilt World*. March/April 1980; June 1982, pp. 52-53.

Dyer, Margie. *Pennsylvania German Quilts*. New York: Goethe House, 1983.

Earle, Alice Morse. *Home Life in Colonial Days*. New York: Macmillan Company, 1898.

Eaton, Allen H. *Handicrafts of the Southern Highlands*. New York: Russell Sage Foundation, 1937.

Echelman, E. M. "Juscht En Deppich," *The Pennsylvania German*. Vol. VII, No. 5, September, 1906, pp. 203-204.

estate inventories, Columbia and Montour counties. 1814-1878; Huntingdon County 1791-1915.

Finley, Ruth E. *Old Patchwork Quilts and the Women Who Made Them*. Philadelphia: J. B. Lippincott & Co., 1929.

Fisher, H. L. *Olden Times: or Pennsylvania Rural Life Some Fifty Years Ago*. York: Fisher Brothers, 1888.

Fitzrandolph, Mavis. *Traditional Quilting. Its Story and Practice*. London: B. T. Batsford, 1954.

Fox, Sandi. *19th Century American Patchwork Quilt*. Tokyo, Japan: The Seibu Museum of Art, 1983.

——————— . *Quilts in Utah/A Reflection of the Western Experience*. n.p., n.d.

——————— . *Small Endearments*. New York: Charles Scribner's Sons, 1985.

Frost, S. Annie. *The Ladies Guide to Needlework, Embroideries, Etc.* 1877.

Fry, Thomas L. *American Quilts/A Handmade Legacy*. Oakland, California: The Oakland Museum, 1981.

Garoutte, Sally, editor. *Uncoverings 1980*. Mill Valley, California: American Quilt Study Group (1981) includes the following articles: Barbara Brackman, "Midwestern Pattern Sources;" Lucille Hilty, "The Passion for Quiltmaking;" Sally Garoutte, "Early Colonial Quilts in a Bedding Context;" Joyce Gross, "Four Twentieth Century Quiltmakers;" Sandra Metzler-Smith, "Quilts in Pomo Culture;" Bets Ramsey, "Design Invention in Country Quilts of Tennessee and Georgia;" Winifred Reddell, "Pieced Lettering on Seven Quilts Dating from 1833 to 1891;" Cuesta Benberry, "Afro-American Women and Quilts: An Introductory Essay;" Jean T. Federico, "White Oak Classification System;" and John L. Oldani, "Archiving and the American Quilt: A Position Paper."

Garoutte, Sally, editor. *Uncoverings 1981*. Mill Valley, California: American Quilt Study Group (1982) includes articles by Katherine R. Koob, "Documenting Quilts by Their Fabrics;" Judy Mathieson, "Some Sources of Design Inspiration for the Quilt Pattern Mariner's Compass;" Dorothy Cozart, "Women and Their Quilts as Portrayed by Some American Authors;" Flavin Glover, "Discovery of the Cedar Heights Quilt Collection;" Marilyn P. Davis, "The Contemporary American Quilter;" Sally Garoutte, "California's First Quilting Party;" Barbara Brackman "Quilts at Chicago's World's Fairs;" Lynn A. Bonfield, "The Production of Cloth, Clothing and Quilts in 19th Century New England Homes;" Mary Katherine Jarrell, "Three Historic Quilts" and Imelda G. DeGraw, "Museum Quilt Collecting."

Garoutte, Sally, editor. *Uncoverings 1982*. Mill Valley, California: American Quilt Study Group (1983) includes the following articles: Tandy Hersh, "Some Aspects of an 1809 Quilt;" Bertha B. Brown, "Cuna Molas: The Geometry of Background Fill;" Ellen F. Eanes, "Nine Related Quilts of Mecklenburg County, 1800-1830;" Nancy J. Rowley, "Red Cross Quilts for the Great War;" Pat Nickols, "String Quilts;" Barbara Brackman, "The Hall/Szabronski Collection at the University of Kansas;" Mary Antoine de Julio, "A Record of a Woman's Work: The Betsy Reynolds Voorhees Collection;" Margaret Malanyn. "Fifteen Dearborn Quilts;" Mary Cross, "The Quilts of Grant Wood's Family and Paintings;" and Sally Garoutte's "Marseilles Quilts and Their Woven Offspring."

Garoutte, Sally, editor. *Uncoverings 1983*. Mill Valley, California: American Quilt Study Group (1984) includes the following articles: Virginia Gunn, "Victorian Silk Template Patchwork in American Periodicals, 1850-1875;" Bets Ramsey, "Recollections of Childhood Recorded in a Tennessee Quilt;" Suzanne Yabsley, "Applique Button Blankets in Northwest Coast Indian Culture;" Nancy Habersat Caudle, "Downeast Country Women: Quilts and Coverlets;" Cuesta Benberry, "White Perspectives of Blacks in Quilts and Related Media;" Diana Church, "The Bayliss Stenciled Quilt;" Laurel Horton, "Nineteenth Century Middle Class Quilts in Macon County, North Carolina;" Barbara Brackman, "A Chronological Index to Pieced Quilt Patterns, 1775-1825;" Margit Reichelt-Jordan, "Patchwork Objects from Around the World," and Katy Christopherson, "Documenting Kentucky's Quilts: An Experiment in Research by Committee."

Garoutte, Sally, editor. *Uncoverings 1984*. Mill Valley, California: American Quilt Study Group (1985) includes the following articles: Nancil B. Burdick, "Talula Gilbert Bottoms and Her Quilts;" James M. Liles, "Dyes in American Quilts Made Before 1930;" Dorothy Cozart, "A Century of Fundraising Quilts: 1860-1960;" Laurel Horton, "South Carolina's Traditional Quilts;" Sandra M. Todaro, "A Family of Texas Quilters and Their Work;" Tandy Hersh, "18th Century Quilted Silk Petticoats Worn in America;" Suellen Meyer, "Characteristics of Missouri-German Quilts;" Louise O. Townsend, "Kansas City Star Quilt Patterns; 1928-1949;" Virginia Gunn, "Crazy Quilts and Outline Quilts: Popular Responses to the Decorative Art/Art Needlework Movement 1876-1893;" and Merikay Waldvogel, "Quilts in the W.P.A. Milwaukee Handicraft Project, 1935-1943."

Garoutte, Sally, editor. *Uncoverings 1985*. Mill Valley, California: American Quilt Study Group (1986) includes the following papers: Gloria Allen, "Bed Coverings: Kent County, Maryland, 1710-1820;" Linda Boynton, "Recent Changes in Amish Quilting Designs;" Sally Garoutte, "Uses of Textiles in Hawaii, 1820-1850;" Virginia Gunn, "Quilts for Union Soldiers in the Civil War;" Bettina Havig, "Missouri: Crossroads of Quilting;" Laurel Horton, "South Carolina Quilts in the Civil War;" Becky Joseph, "Traditions and Innovation in Kentucky Quilts and Yogyakarta Batiks;" Erma Kirkpatrick, "Quilts, Quiltmaking and the *Progressive Farmer*: 1886-1935", and Jeannette Lasansky, "The Hap in Pennsylvania's 19th and 20th Century Quiltmaking Traditions."

Garrad, Larch S. "Quilting and Patchwork in the Isle of Man," *A Journal of Ethnological Studies/Folk Life,* 1979, pp. 39-48.

Garvan, Beatrice B. and Charles F. Hummel. *The Pennsylvania Germans/ A Celebration of Their Arts 1683-1853*. Philadelphia: Philadelphia Museum of Arts, 1983.

Gibbons, Phebe Earle. *Pennsylvania Dutch and Other Essays*. Philadelphia: J. B. Lippincott & Co., 1882.

Godey's Lady's Book. 1830-1897.

Good Housekeeping. 1885-1940.

Graeff, Marie Knorr. *Pennsylvania German Quilts*. Home Craft Course, Vol. XIV., 1964.

Grandmother Clark's & Authentic Early American Patchwork Quilts. St. Louis, Missouri: W. L. M. Clark, 1932.

"The Great American Quilt Classics—Rose of Sharon." *Quilters Newsletter Magazine*. October 1978, pp. 15-15.

Hagerman, Betty. "The Great American Quilt Classics—Sunbonnets." *Quilters Newsletter Magazine*. April 1979, pp. 6-9.

_____. "A Meeting of the Sunbonnet Children." Baldwin City, Kansas: Betty Hagerman, 1979.

Hale, Sarah. *Mrs. Hale's Receipts for the Million*. Philadelphia: Peterson, 1857.

Hall, Carrie A. and Rose G. Kretsinger. *The Romance of the Patchwork Quilt in America*. Caldwell, Idaho: Caxton Printers Ltd., Bonanza Books, 1935.

Harney, Andy Leon. "WPA Handicrafts Rediscovered." *Historic Preservation Magazine*. July-September 1973, pp. 10-15.

Havig, Bettina. *Missouri Heritage Quilts*. Paducah, Kentucky: American Quilters Society, 1986.

Holstein, Jonathan. *Abstract Design in American Quilts*. New York: Whitney Museum of Art, 1971.

_____. *Kentucky Quilts 1800-1900/The Kentucky Quilt Project*. New York: Pantheon Books, 1982.

_____. *The Pieced Quilt/An American Design Tradition*. Boston: New York Graphic Society; Little, Brown and Company. 1973.

Horton, Laurel and Lynn Robertson Myers. *Social Fabric/South Carolina's Traditional Quilts*. Charleston: McKissick Museum, 1985.

House Beautiful. 1897-1930.

Ickis, Marguerite. *The Standard Book of Quilt Making and Collecting*. New York: Dover Publications Inc., 1959 (rpt.) 1949.

Instructions For Patchwork. n.p.: J. F. Ingalls, 1884.

Irwin, John Rice. *A People and Their Quilts*. Exton, PA: Schiffer Publishing Ltd, 1984.

Jeffery, G. G. *Rugs & Quilts,* London: Oxford University Press, 1943.

Johnson, Geraldine. "Plain and Fancy': The Socioeconomics of Blue Ridge Quilts." *Appalachian Journal*. Autumn 1982, pp. 12-35.

Katzenburg, Dena S. *Baltimore Album Quilts*. Baltimore: The Baltimore Museum of Art, 1980.

_____. *The Great American Cover-Up/Counterpanes of the Eighteenth and Nineteenth Centuries*. Baltimore: The Baltimore Museum of Art, 1971.

Keyser, Alan G. "Beds, Bedding, Bedsteads and Sleep," *The Quarterly of Pennsylvania German Society,* The Pennsylvania German Society: Breinigsville, Pennsylvania, October, 1978, pp. 1-28.

King, Elizabeth. *Quilting*. New York: Leisure League of America, 1934.

Kiracofe, Roderick and Michael Kile. *The Quilt Digest*. San Francisco: Kirakofe and Kile, 1983-1986.

Kyser, Pat Flynn. "Pieces & Patches." *Quilt World*. April 1979, pp. 4-7.

Ladies' Art Company Catalogs, St. Louis, Missouri: Ladies' Art Company, 1898-1928.

Ladies Home Journal, 1892-1907.

Ladies Manual of Fancy Work. Vol. 3 No. 3, April 1903.

Ladies Magazine. 1834-1836.

Ladies National Magazine. 1844-1845, 1880-1881.

Ladies Register and Housewife's Almanack. 1844.

Lasansky, Jeannette, editor, *In the Heart of Pennsylvania/Symposium Papers,* Lewisburg, Pennsylvania: Oral Traditions Project, 1986, with "Quiltmaking within Women's Needlework Repertoire" by Susan Swan; "The American Block Quilt" by Jonathan Holstein; "What Distinguishes a Pennsylvania Quilt" by Patricia T. Herr; "A Century of Old Order Amish Quiltmaking in Mifflin County" by Eve Wheatcroft Granick, "Quilting in the Goschenhoppen" by Nancy Roan; "The Typical Versus the Unusual/Distortion of Time" by Jeannette Lasansky; "The Needlework of an American Lady/ Social History in Quilts" by Ricky Clark; "Various Aspects of Dating Quilts" by Gail van der Hoof; "Paradigms of Scarcity and Abundance/The Quilt as an Artifact of the Industrial Revolution" by Rachel Maines, and "The Display, Care, and Conservation of Old Quilts" by Virginia Gunn.

Leslie, Eliza. *American Girl's Book* or *Occupation for Play Hours*. New York: R. Worthington, 16th ed. 1879.

_____. *The House Book*. Philadelphia: Cary & Hart, 1840.

letters of Eliza Reader, Mary Eby, Lizzie Twist, and others. Perry County, 1868-1897, private collection.

Lipsett, Linda Otto. *Remember Me/Women & Their Friendship Quilts*. San Francisco: Quilt Digest Press, 1985.

MacDowell, Marsha, "Michigan Quilts" *Michigan History,* July-August 1984, pp. 32-34.

McElwain, Mary A. *Notes on Applied Work and Patchwork*. London: His Majesty's Stationery Office, 1949.

_____. *Notes on Quilting*. London: His Majesty's Stationery Office, 1949.

_____. *The Romance of Village Quilts*. Walworth, Wisconsin: n.p., 1936.

McKendry, Ruth. *Traditional Quilts and Bed Coverings*. Toronto: Van Nostrand Reinhold Company, 1979.

McKim, Ruby. *One Hundred and One Patchwork Patterns*. Independence, Missouri: McKim Studios, 1931.

McMorris, Penny. *Crazy Quilts*. New York: E. P. Dutton, 1984.

Merriam, Mary. *Quilts*. Deerfield, Mass.: Pocumtuck Valley Memorial Association, 1985.

Montgomery, Florence. *Printed Textiles/English and American Cottons and Linens.* New York: The Viking Press, 1970.

Mountain Artisans. Providence, Rhode Island: Rhode Island School of Design, 1970.

Mountain Mist quilt wrappers, 1931-1939.

The Mountain Mist Blue Book of Quilts. Cincinnati, Ohio: Stearns and Foster Company, 1937.

The National Stockman and Farmer or *The Pennsylvania Stockman and Farmer,* 1884-1928.

Needlecraft, 1900-1928.

New Jersey Quilters/A Timeless Tradition. Morristown, New Jersey: Morristown Museum of Arts and Sciences, 1982.

New York Times. 1861-1865.

Nicoll, Jessica F. *Quilted for Friends/Delaware Valley Signature Quilts, 1840-1855.* Winterthur, Delaware. The Henry Francis DuPont Winterthur Museum, 1986.

North Carolina Country Quilts. Chapel Hill, North Carolina: The Ackland Art Museum, 1978.

"Old Dutch Girl." *Quilt World Omnibook.* Summer 1979, pp. 40-41.

"The Oldest Quilt Business in the U.S.A." *Ladies Circle of Patchwork Quilts.* #10, p. 6-11.

"Patchwork in the North East." Gateshead, England: Tyne and Wear County Council Museums Service, n.d.

Patriot & Union (Harrisburg). 1861-1865.

Orlofsky, Patsy and Myron. *Quilts in America.* New York: McGraw-Hill Book Company, 1974.

Pennsylvania Quilts, One Hundred Years, 1830-1930. Philadelphia: Moore College of Art, 1978.

Pennsylvania Telegraph (Harrisburg). 1861-1865.

Peterson, Harold. *American Interiors from Colonial Times to the Late Victorians.* New York: Charles Scribner's Sons, 1971.

Peterson's Magazine. 1843-1891.

Peto, Florence, *American Quilts and Coverlets/A History of a Charming Native Art Together With a Manual of Instruction for Beginners.* New York: Chanticleer Press, 1949.

————————— . *Historic Quilts.* New York: American Historical Company, 1939.

Pettit, Florence H. *America's Printed and Painted Fabrics 1600-1900.* New York: Hastings House, 1970.

Pullan, Mrs. *Ladies Manual of Fancy Work.* New York: Dick Fitzgerald, Publishers, 1859.

"Quilting in the North East." Gateshead, England: Tyne and Wear County Council Museums Service, n.d.

"Quiltmaking Pioneer, Scioto Imhoff Danner." *Quilters Newsletter Magazine,* June 1973, p. 6.

Quilts from Cinncinnati Collections, Cincinnati: Cincinnati Art Museum, 1985.

"Quilts in Indianapolis Museums." *Ladies Circle Patchwork Quilts.* #10, p. 30.

Ramsey, Bets and Marikay Waldvogel. *The Quilts of Tennessee/Images of Domestic Life Prior to 1930.* Nashville, Tennessee: Rutledge Hill Press, 1986.

Roan, Nancy and Ellen J. Gehret. *Just A Quilt or Juscht en Deppich.* Green Lane, Pennsylvania: Goschenhoppen Historians, 1984.

Robacker, Earl F. *Old Stuff in Up-Country Pennsylvania.* New York: A. S. Barnes and Company, 1973.

Robertson, Elizabeth Wells. *American Quilts.* New York: Studio Publications, Inc., 1948.

"Rose Kretsinger—Applique Artist." *Quilters Newsletter Magazine.* December 1977, pp. 24, 25, 29.

"Ruby Short McKim." *Quilters Newsletter Magazine.* December 1976, pp. 14-15.

Safford, Carleton, L. and Bishop, Robert. *American Quilts and Coverlets.* New York: E. P. Dutton & Company, Inc., 1972.

Sater, Joel. *The Patchwork Quilt.* Ephrata, Pennsylvania: Science Press, 1981.

Schwoeffermann, Catherine. *Threaded Memories: A Family Quilt Collection.* Binghamton, New York: Roberson Center, 1984.

Sears Century of Progress in Quiltmaking. Chicago: Sears, Roebuck & Co., 1934.

Sears Roebuck catalogs. 1897 and 1902.

Sexton, Carlie. *Early American Quilts.* Southampton, New York: Crackerbarrel Press, 1924.

————————— . *Yesterdays Quilts in Homes of Today.* Des Moines, Iowa: Meredith Publishing Company, 1930.

Shirer, Marie, "My Great-Great-Aunt Made Quilts." *Quilters Newsletter Magazine.* February 1980, pp. 12-15.

Silber, Merry. *World of Quilts at Meadowbrook Hall.* Rochester, Michigan: Oakland University, 1983.

Smith, Wilene. *Quilt Patterns and Index to Kansas City Star Patterns.* Wichita, Kansas: Wilene Smith, 1985.

Snow, Virginia. *Quilting Designs.* Elgin, Illinois: Virginia Snow Studios, n.d.

Star of the North (Bloomsburg). 1861-1865.

Stoddard, Ada C. "A Story of Patchwork Old and New." *Quilt World.* April 1976, pp. 24-25.

Swan, Susan Burrows. "Household Textiles" *The Art of the Pennsylvania Germans.* New York: W. W. Norton & Co., 1983.

Tenet, Rose. "Irish Patchwork 1800-1900." *Quilt World Omnibook.* Summer 1981, pp. 4-5.

Townsend, Louise O. "Eveline Foland, Quilt Pattern Illustrator." *Quilters Newsletter Magazine.* April 1985, pp. 20-22.

The Universal Entertainer. 1743-1753.

Ward, Anne. "Quilting in the North of England," *A Journal of the Society for Folk Life Studies,* 1966, pp. 75-81.

Webster, Marie D. *Quilts: Their Story and How to Make Them.* New York: Doubleday, Page and Company, 1915.

White, Margaret E. *Quilts and Counterpanes in the Newark Museum.* Newark, New Jersey: The Newark Museum, 1948.

Woodward, Thomas K. and Blanche Greenstein. *Crib Quilts and Other Small Wonders.* New York: E. P. Dutton, 1981.

Works Progress Administration Files. Archives of the Pennsylvania Historical Museum Commission, Harrisburg.

Yabsley, Suzanne. *Texas Quilts, Texas Women.* College Station, Texas: Texas A & M University, 1984.

Documentation Day Informants

Albright, Janette M., Landisburg; Albright, Joseph H., Mifflinville; Anderson, Jean G., Huntingdon; Arey, Geraldine, Mildred; Arndt, Marian B., Harrisburg; Aughey, Lura L., Mifflintown; Avery, Mrs. Gene, Dushore; Baker, Anne E., Huntingdon; Baker, Mrs. Marian Neff, Alexandria; Baker, Ruth W., Laporte; Barber, Myrtle, Grantville; Barns, Gladys, Millerstown; Baumunk, Caroline, Shunk; Beaver, Kathryn B., Millerstown; Bell, Marjorie, Petersburg; Berger, Ruth Thomas, Sunbury; Berrier, Mary, Huntingdon; Bertolette, Edna, Camp Hill; Betts, Carolyn Frymire, Trout Run; Bingaman, Mrs. Louise, Milton; Bishop, Frances R., Harrisburg; Bitner, Galen and Janet A., Carlisle; Blain, Mrs. Anne, Danville; Blaine, Pearl, Newport; Bollinger, Julie, Selinsgrove; Booher, Mrs. Frank, Rock Hill Furnace; Bower, Scott E., Berwick; Bowman, Betty J., Carlisle; Bowman, Eleanor L., Camp Hill; Brandt, C. Richard, Mechanicsburg; Braucht, Charles, Spring Mills; Braunbeck, Rebecca, Trout Run; Breitenbach, Geraldine P., Carlisle; Brodnick, Mary E. Shearer, East Waterford; Brown, Barbara W., Colchester, CT.; Brown, Ruth, Huntingdon; Brubaker, Ellen S., Halifax; Bryner, Victoria, Carlisle; Buttington, Darla, Harrisburg; Byers, Marjorie A., Millerstown.

Catherman, Mary, Milton; Cavanaugh, Mrs. Lester, Mifflin; Cerra, Margaret N., Lewistown; Clouse, Jerry A., Hummelstown; Cohick, Fern, Enhaut; Collier, Walter, Newport; Cook, Louise, Huntingdon; Corbin, Joan H., Huntingdon; Corbin, Mrs. R., Huntingdon; Covert, Phyllis, Three Springs; Craner, Elaine, Mifflintown; Croll, John and Betty, Middletown; Crook, Martha, Hummelstown; Crosby, Adelaide B., Huntingdon; Cruet, William, Huntingdon; Cunningham, Randy, Huntingdon; Cupp, Lawrence Heisler, New Bloomfield; Darr, Miriam, Alexandria; DeForest, Betty C., Three Springs; Devanney, Wilma H., Mechanicsburg; Dietz, Mrs. D. Stoner, Camp Hill; Drake, Sara E., Camp Hill; Driskell, Julia, Bloomsburg; Ebright, Edith, Mifflintown; Edburgh, Karl and Mary, Berwick; Elsesser, Alma, Lewistown; Epler, Elizabeth, Orangeville; Ernst, Paul R., Lewisburg; Esh, Marjorie R., Mifflintown; Eshenour, Erma, Elliottsburg; Eyler, Ron, Camp Hill.

Faesel, Arlene S., Carlisle; Fahrienger, Mr. and Mrs. James, Laporte; Felix, Peggy Ann, Berwick; Fenstermacher, Mrs. Mildred, Milton; Fiester, Helen K., Muncy Valley; Fisher, Janet M., Millerstown; Fleagle, Gary and Karen, Harrisburg; Flower, Mrs. James D., Carlisle; Focht, Mary, Sunbury; Fogleman, Mr. and Mrs. Robert A., Port Royal; Ford, Dona P., Saltillo; Ford, Marie, Saltillo; Frazier, Mildred, Muncy Valley; Frey, Leona, Shunk; Fritz, Natalie, Newport; Frohwirth, Helen K., Hershey; Frymoyer, Esther, Cocolamus; Fultz, Edna C., Dover; Funk, Sylvia, Shiremanstown; Gabos, Eva, Mifflinville; Geltz, Elizabeth, Mechanicsburg; George, Dora P., Harrisburg; Gerhardt, Lyndall L., Boiling Springs; Gibbs, Evelyn O., Harrisburg; Gilsen, Barbara N., Port Royal; Gloss, Alverta, Honey Grove; Good, Lenna, Wapwallopen; Goodyear, Virginia D., Mt. Holly Springs; Goshorn, Eleanor Crull, East Waterford; Grausam, Amy, Danville; Greenland, Emily M., Three Springs; Greenleaf, Frances H., Huntingdon; Gross, Rosie, Lewistown; Grove, Marguerite E., Carlisle; Guerin, Jane, Huntingdon; Guss, Mrs. Karl E., Mifflintown.

Hagenbuch, Hortense, Berwick; Hanawalt, Martha M., Huntingdon; Harrington, Barbara, Huntingdon; Harshbarger, Mrs. William, Alexandria; Hartman, Mrs. Linda D., Harrisburg; Hartslog Heritage Museum, Alexandria; Hatton, Mrs. Miriam, Mildred; Hawn, Mrs. George, Boalsburg; Hench, Faye Shumaker, Enola; Hench, Patricia, Carlisle; Henry, Helen G., Mifflin; Henry, Mrs. John P., Sr., Honey Grove; Henry, Mary S., Port Royal; Herald, Jane Youngman, Turbotville; Hersh, Tandy, Carlisle; Hileman, Mr. William, Bloomsburg; Hockenbrock, Joanne, Winfield; Holcombe, Pauline C., Dushore; Holsinger, Virginia M., Huntingdon; Hoover, Donna Lee, Mechanicsburg; Hoover, Wanda, Etters; Horting, Julia B., Newport; Horton, Darlene, Three Springs; Hostettler, Klara P., Mifflintown; Hottenstein, Helen, Forksville; Houseweart, Miriam, Benton; Hower, Letitia, Mexico; Hughes, Henrietta Longenberger, Berwick; Hulbert, Mildred, Camp Hill; Hummel, Ruth, Huntingdon; Hunter, Susie K., Muncy Valley; Isett, Mary Stewart, Huntingdon.

Kauffman, Marie B., Mifflintown; Kazarise, Pauline, Huntingdon; Kell, Mrs. J. Ernest, Mifflintown; Kelley, Mrs. Arlene L., Mifflintown; Kelley, Mrs. Orville G., Marysville; Kelley, Phoebe, Dushore; Kelley, Raymond and Pauline, Dushore; Kemmler, Margaret A., Burnt Cabins; Kemp, Louise, Lewisburg; Kern, Lloyd, Harrisburg; Kershner, Helen H., Mifflin; Kingsborough, Ann, Loysville; Kinter, Mrs. Herman C., Newport; Kitchen, June, Laporte; Klinger, Anzonetta J., Camp Hill; Kocher, Eileen, Berwick; Kocher, Ruth, Danville; Kosco, Betty S., Carlisle; Kutz, Earl, Jr., New Cumberland; Laite, Berkly, Shippensburg; Laubach, Mrs. David E., Berwick; Lauver, Annette, Mifflintown; Lauver, Helen, Mifflintown; Leach, Colleen Cook, Mifflintown; Leamer, Donna, McConnellstown; Leffard, Stanley, Huntingdon; Lehman, Lucy G., Port Royal; Leiter, Mary Anne, Duncannon; Leitzel, Gladys, Cocolamus; Leverentz, Shirley, Harrisburg; Lewis, Mr. and Mrs. Dwight, Hillsgrove; Leyder, Delores, New Bloomfield; Lightner, Doris Jane, Landisburg; Lightner, Lester Irvine, Landisburg; Lightner, Mary, Huntingdon; Lightner, Neil Irvine, Landisburg; Lightner, Neila Irene, Mechanicsburg; Lilley, Mrs. John C., Boiling Springs; Linn, Ruth Ann, Newport; Ohler, LaRue, Huntingdon; Litzenberger, Mr. and Mrs. Don, Huntingdon; Long, Jean P., Three Springs; Long, Patricia Zug, Lutherville, MD; Longenberger, Pauline, Berwick; Lontz, Mary Belle and Hattie, Milton; Louder, Mr. and Mrs. Robert E., Huntingdon; Lynn, Carol D., Alexandria; Lynn, Edna, Catawissa; Lykens, Letty M., New Cumberland.

Mader, Doris Wenrick, Harrisburg; Marbain, Barbara H., Mechanicsburg; Marhefka, Jane, New Bloomfield; Martin, Cheryl D., Lewisberry; Marzolf, Mrs. Marjorie W., Carlisle; Matthews, Jane, Lemoyne; Mauck, Eleanor M., Harrisburg; Melton, Mrs. Lucille, New Kingstown; Metcalf, Estella R., Carlisle; McCarty, M., Dushore; McClafferty, Susanne W., Mechanicsburg; McClain, Mrs. Cheryl Ann Gross, Huntingdon; McClintock, Mrs. George H., Jr., New Cumberland; McCloskey, J. Patrick, Mt. Union; McCracken, Becky, Huntingdon; McLane, Rozella, Mechanicsburg; Miller, Alice G., Bloomsburg; Miller, Mr. and Mrs. Daniel M., Huntingdon; Miller, Maryanne, Berwick; Miller, Pat, Huntingdon; Moeller, Grace, Harrisburg; Moist Family, Mifflintown; Molyneus, Mrs. Phyllis A., Forksville; Moore, Myra Worley, Milton;

Mordan, Joyce, Danville; Morrison, Alta, Newport; Morrison, Marie, Newport; Moser, Marie B., Huntingdon; Mueller, Janet C., Forksville; Muggio, Darby, Dauphin; Muller, Joan M., Wapwallopen; Meyers, Patricia Dugan, Harrisburg; Nee, Mrs. Floyd, Alexandria; Nelson, Mr. and Mrs. W. Irvin, Newville; Nesbitt, John Franklin, Mechanicsburg; Noll, Edith, Newport; Novi, Leah M., Carlisle; O'Neill, Mrs. John, Bloomsburg; Orner, Caroline, Newville; Otstot, John, Carlisle; Otten, Mrs. Adolf C., Dushore.

Park, Isabel P., Three Springs; Payne, Ethel L., Mifflinville; Pechart, Ella, Shippensburg; Peduzzi, Mrs. Carl, Mt. Union; Persons, Betty H., Mt. Holly Springs; Phelleps, Rose Mary, Camp Hill; Ployer, Mary Jane, New Cumberland; Pope, Mr. and Mrs. Jeff, Danville; Port, Joyce B., Mt. Union; Priest, Janet L., Carlisle; Railing, Ellena, Carlisle; Reed, George K., Camp Hill; Reisinger, Earl and Linda, Mechanicsburg; Rexrode, Winifred W., Shiremanstown; Rhodes, Marie, Bloomsburg; Rife, Jane S., Dauphin; Rice, Martha, Newport; Rishel, Ann, Alexandria; Roadarmel, Hellen, Bloomsburg; Robb, Vera, Huntingdon; Robinson, Virginia E., Rockhill Furnace; Rogers, Barbara, Harrisburg; Roley, Sarah, Carlisle; Roth, G. Book, Carlisle; Rovegno, Evelyn B., Carlisle; Rubery, Grace, Berwick; Rupert, Ruth, Huntingdon; Ryan, William, Bloomsburg.

Sailhamer, Candy, Carlisle; Sandel, Esther D., Bloomsburg; Sandel, Kathryn and George F., Hummelstown; Schlegel, Barbara H., Mifflintown; Schubert, Susan A., Harrisburg; Sechler, Howard, Danville; Shaffer, Mrs. James, Bloomsburg; Shaffer, Miss Jennifer L., Bloomsburg; Shaffer, Mary Lou, Forksville; Shedd, Nancy, Petersburg; Shelley, Laentena, Port Royal; Shelley, Thelma, McAlisterville; Shellhamer, Louise, Camp Hill; Shireman, Ruth, Middletown; Shoemaker, Etta, Laporte; Shope, Mrs. Letha, Huntingdon; Shusser, Carol Ann, Nescopeck; Shultz, Elizabeth J., Berwick; Shultz, Mrs. Sarah B., Boiling Springs; Sidle, Barbara, Bowmansdale; Sieber, Anna, Thompsontown; Sigler, Reba H., Mifflintown; Silver Spring Presbyterian Church, Mechanicsburg; Singer, Nora Ella, Mifflintown; Slear, Gary, Lewisburg; Smith, Florence M., Blair; Smith, Florence B., Eagles Mere; Smith, Isabel, Mifflintown; Smith, Jean, Bellefonte; Smith, Joan, Harrisburg; Smith, John & Betty, Three Springs; Smith, Mrs. Lester E., Newport; Smith, Nancy, Camp Hill; Smith, Ralph L., Newport; Smith, Stella, Shade Gap; Smith, Thelma, Hummelstown; Snyder, Mrs. Charles, Jr., Mifflinburg; Snyder, LaRue, Camp Hill; Snyder, Mary, Mechanicsburg; Snyder, Nedra, Laporte; Snyder, Mr. and Mrs. Phillip, Laporte; Soberick, Jayne, Berwick; Soberick, Kim M., Berwick; Soberick, Kristi A., Berwick; Soberick, Lois M., Berwick; Spangler, Annabella C., Harrisburg; Springer, Edith, Middletown; Stabnau, Mary, Newville; Stailey, Lori, Harrisburg; Stampes, Snolia, Carlisle; St. Clair, Carol, Sonestown; Stephens, Annabelle, Newport; Stertine, Annie E. Library, Lewisberry; Stimmel, Mrs. William C., Port Royal; Stoner, Mary Martha, Mifflintown; Stouffer, Anne, Carlisle; Stuter, Amy, Mifflintown; Sulteaberger, Florence M., Carlisle; Swanger, Ruth, Milton; Swarmer, Nancy L., Carlisle; Swartz, Abbe Pearl, Mifflintown; Swartz, Sara E., Mifflintown.

Taylor, Mr. and Mrs. Newton C., Huntingdon; Taylor, Mrs. Paul, Newport; Temple, Earl, Unityville; Thomas, Mrs. Harold, Dushore; Thorpe, Lydia M., Harrisburg; Toothaker, Florence R., Dushore; Tressler, Resta, Newport; Trick, Anna, Dushore; Trout, Helen, Newport; Van Ormer, Mildred, McAlisterville; Vicars, Violet E., McAlisterville; Von Neida, Myrtle, Richfield; Wagner, Darlene, Harrisburg; Walker, Harriet T., Newport; Walters, Mrs. Sara, Mifflintown; Waters, Lily, Alexandria, VA.; Waters, Ruth, Mifflin; Watson, Jane Town, Mifflinburg; Weaver, Arlene C., Halifax; Weller, Kathryn D., Berwick; Wentzel, Arlene C., Carlisle; Wert, Sharon, Millerstown; Wertz, Miss Diana, Millerstown; Whitekettle, Pauline, Newport; Wilson, George and Margaret, Huntingdon; Wilson, Levinia H., Mifflintown; Wilt, Gail Eby Isett, Huntingdon; Winder, Rosemary L., Mifflintown; Wolf, Virginia L., Mifflintown; Wright, Helen G., New Bloomfield; Wrightstone, G. Robert, Mechanicsburg; Yohn, Lillian Y., Port Royal; Young, Mrs. Marion D., Dushore; Yow, Harriet, Trout Run; Zaner, Cora, Dushore; Zawadski, Clara, Shiremanstown; Zimmerman, Catherine, Port Royal.

INDEX